A Natural History and Field Guide to Australia's Top End

Penny van Oosterzee
Ian Morris
Diane Lucas
Noel Preece

GECKO
BOOKS

First published by Gecko Books in 2014

Publisher: Gecko Books
6 Moss Avenue
Marleston SA. 5033 Australia
Email: sales@jbbooks.com.au

National Library of Australia Cataloguing-in-Publication entry:

Authors: Penny van Oosterzee, Ian Morris, Diane Lucas, Noel Preece
A Natural History and Field Guide to Australia's Top End
ISBN: 9780 9924 20833
Dewey Number: 578.0994295
Subjects: Natural history--Northern Territory--Australia's Top End
                 Habitat (Ecology)--Northern Territory--Australia's Top End
                 Botany--Northern Territory--Australia's Top End
                 Zoology--Northern Territory--Australia's Top End
                 Australia's Top End and Darwin Region (N.T.)--Description and travel
Notes: Includes Index
            References for further reading

Layout and Design: by Jacinda Brown - Chook Shed Studio

Printed by: Asia Pacific Offset
The paper used in this book is sourced from sustainably managed European forests.

Extra photographic contributions:

Diane Lucas (DL) 59 Photographs initialed throughout the book
Jacinda Brown (JB) 110 Photographs initialed throughout the book
Some of Jacinda's photographs were taken at the Territory Wildlife Park as part of their Artist in Residence program.
Jeremy Russell-Smith (JRS) pages 185x2,190, 38, 39, 36, 37, 116
Trevor Collins (TC) pages; 115,119, 161, 162, 163
Carol Palmer (CP) page; 182 x 3
Peter Whitehead (PW) page; 57
Peter Murray (PM) pages; 10,14,15,16
Russell Dempster (RD) pages; 86, 111 x 2
Jackson Marshall (JM) page; 88
Roland Tanglao (RT) page; 14, http://commons.wikimedia.org/wiki/File:Tyrrell_Ichthyosaur.jpg
Jens Peterson (JP) page; 171, http://commons.wikimedia.org/wiki/File:Hapalochlaena_lunulata2.JPG

Maps and Diagrams:

Vegetation Map (page 4) - Noel Preece
Diagrams (pages 11, 15, 36 & 151) - compiled by Diane Lucas and Jacinda Brown
Ichthyosaur page 14 Heinrich Harder http://commons.wikimedia.org/wiki/File:Ichthyosaurs.jpg
Plesiosaur page 14 William Buckland http://commons.wikimedia.org/wiki/File:Anningplesiosaur.png
Graph on page 34 taken from Bureau of Meteorology NT website showing cyclone intensities from 1963 - 2006

Acknowledgements

We wish to thank and acknowledge the Traditional Owners, and trust that this small book allows visitors and local residents to better appreciate and understand the Darwin region's outstanding natural values.

We are enormously grateful to the many people who have contributed to the development of this beautiful book, including staff of the: NT Herbarium, and for use of Milton Andrew's diagrams, and photos from the Herbarium collection; NT Parks and Wildlife for information and maps; NT Reference Library and the Museum and Art Gallery of the NT for essential research assistance; Darwin City Council for help with maps. We also thank Jackson Marshall for editing some reptile text, Jeremy Russell-Smith for some text edits, Clive Garland for some bird edits and Cameron Yates for initial mapping assistance. Peter Murray kindly allowed us to use diagrams and photos from his 1985 and 1987 marine fossil publications.

While the photos throughout the book are taken mostly by Ian Morris from his extensive and wonderful collection, we also thank the following people for contributing their photos: Diane Lucas (DL), Jacinda Brown (JB), Jeremy Russell-Smith (JRS), Trevor Collins (TC), Carol Palmer (CP), Peter Whitehead (PW), Russell Dempster (RD) and Jackson Marshall (JM).

Jacinda Brown from Chook Shed Studio applied her creative skill in providing the stunning layout and design.

The local tourist shops and bookshops in Darwin provided the encouragement to finally make the decision to compile the book.

JB books provided their vision and encouragement to proceed with the book.

Dedicated to families and country.

Contents

Introduction;
Unfamiliar Theatre

Cosmopolitan Darwin is Australia's most extraordinary city. Deep within the tropics, Darwin is closer to the exotic east Indonesian spice islands than to central Australia's Alice Springs. Everything about the Darwin region reflects this exciting blend of Asia and Australia. Its leafy streets and pockets of monsoon forests hug the opal-coloured Timor Sea, yet are flanked by tall eucalypt forests. Migrating waders sweep across Asia to feed in Top End wetlands, producing a cacophony of sound not unlike the hubbub of multicultural Mindil Beach markets. In the tall forests, magnificent tree-rats - ancient immigrants from Asia - live side by side with marsupials originating in Australia.

The Top End environment is one born of extremes. The spectacular storms and monsoonal deluges alternate with dry-season droughts that may last for more than eight months. In between, from November to January, Darwin lives up to its reputation as the lightning capital of the world with a light and sound event of universal proportions.

The Darwin region is nestled within the wet/dry tropics and its habitats, animals and plants are representative of the entire Top End. This book provides not only a window on the Top End but also an understanding of the dynamics of the wet/dry tropics which is characterised by a belt of forests and woodlands extending from the Kimberley in the west to eastern Queensland

As well as providing an extensive field guide to the habitats and commonly seen animals and plants of the Top End including marine environments, the book has informative explanations of the geological history of the region, its biogeography, climate (with a field guide to the clouds) habitats and seasons.

PART ONE: The Top End

East Alligator river winds across the floodplains, near Gunbalanja.

CHAPTER ONE

Window into the past; the Geology of the Top End

The Darwin region contains a generous slice of the geological history of the Top End. Beginning with the ancient boulder-strewn, rugged hills near Rum Jungle, which are about 2,500 - 2,700 million (2.5 to 2.7 billion) years old - older than most places on Earth - there are also elements which are almost the youngest, such as the "chenier" beach ridges along the beaches surrounding Darwin, which can be as young as 700 years. In fact, the famous coastal plains with their abundant wildlife surrounding Darwin, and nearby in Kakadu, are no older than 7,000 years.

Vegetation map of the Darwin region

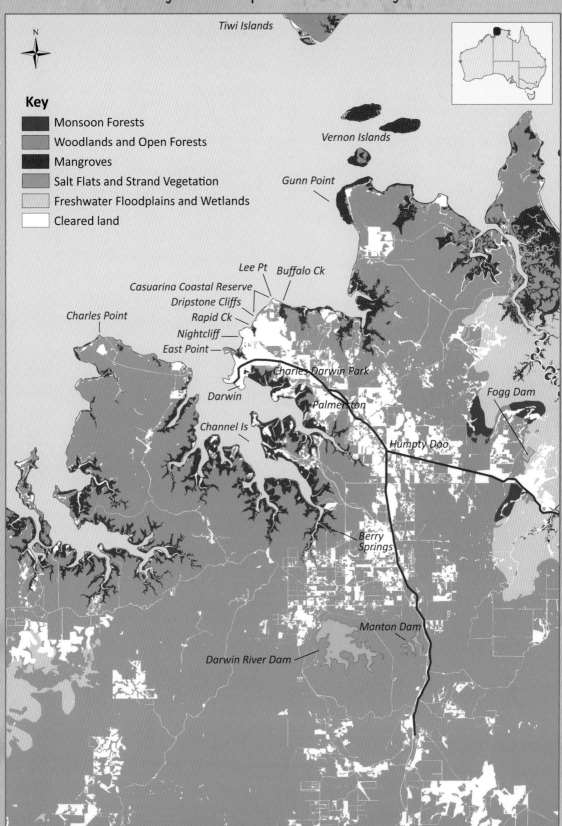

Key

- Monsoon Forests
- Woodlands and Open Forests
- Mangroves
- Salt Flats and Strand Vegetation
- Freshwater Floodplains and Wetlands
- Cleared land

Tiwi Islands

Vernon Islands

Gunn Point

Lee Pt   Buffalo Ck

Casuarina Coastal Reserve

Dripstone Cliffs

Charles Point

Rapid Ck

Nightcliff

East Point

Charles Darwin Park

Fogg Dam

Darwin

Palmerston

Channel Is

Humpty Doo

Berry
Springs

Manton Dam

Darwin River Dam

If you know how to read them, rocks can tell the story of a place. Sometimes the writing is rubbed out, sometimes it is big and bold, and other times very subtle. The rocks underlying the Darwin region are so old that they were deposited when life was little more than single-celled animals swimming in primordial seas. This flight through geological history provides an underpinning to the main landscapes we see today (see map opposite page).

The oldest rocks are dated at about 2700 million years. And even these age-worn rocks trap evidence of an earlier event, having been deformed and tightly folded through at least one mountain building episode. These formed when two tectonic plates of the Earth, one of which contained embryonic Australia, collided, heaping the rock at the plate edges into mountains. Heaved above the sea, the land was leveled by erosion for 500 million years. To put this time-frame into perspective, 500 million years is the time it has taken the very first jawless fish to evolve into mammals and primates such as us.

Rocky outcrop Finniss Valley Batchelor

This lifeless landscape lay near a shallow sea with inlets and lagoons, in which mounds of cyanobacteria, single-celled early plant colonies known as stromatolites, were growing. At about this time, 2200 million years ago, a rift-valley developed. Rift-valleys are the surface expression of the boundary of two of the Earth's giant plates, beginning to rift apart. Today this rift-valley is known as the Pine Creek Geosyncline (meaning, literally, geological trough). This vast, lake-sprinkled valley - resembling the rift-valley of east Africa - stretched from Kakadu to the Kimberley.

Djabiluku outlier system, part of the Kakadu escarpment

Ranger Uranium Mine, with escarpment in the background, Kakadu.

Over millions of years, the rift valley deepened and broadened, trapping 14,000 metres of sediment, which was stripped from the already old hills and mountains of the surrounding environment. The first layer of sediment, dated at the base of the Ranger Uranium Mine, near the township of Jabiru, was deposited at about 2200 million to 2000 million years ago, as alluvial fans brought down by rivers. The alluvial fans graded to a broad continental shelf to the north and north-east, over which the sea was rising, depositing sandstone, claystone and limestone. Nearby submarine volcanoes oozed lava at the tectonic plate, or continental margin boundary.

A period of uplift followed, allowing erosion once again to strip the region to a plain, which the sea again claimed, leaving its calling card as layers of sandstone, claystone and limestone.

Relentless drifting over the surface of the Earth saw the rifting process cease, and the region finally slumped against a submarine trough where one of the Earth's tectonic plates was plunging underneath the plate on which the Top End drifted. The collision crumpled the Top End into lofty mountains once again.

Volcanoes, like the ones to our north today in Indonesia (where the same process of plate subduction is occurring), exploded ash and tuff over the earth's surface. If Top End rocks could talk, this would probably be the most memorable event of their existence to date. It is known as the Top End Orogeny by geologists and the evidence in the rocks indicates that it resulted in the birth of a massive, probably Himalayan-sized, mountain range - now wiped away by time and erosion. This mountain building episode, starting at about 1870 million years ago, endured for about 90 million years.

It was during this period that furnace-hot volcanoes and boiling groundwater distilled uranium and other ores from older sediments and deposited them in rich layers or as veins in other rocks. These ore bodies would later be mined by humans who were yet to evolve from the single-celled animals swimming in the seas at that time.

Several tens of millions of years of erosion tore down the mountains of the Top End Orogeny, until the seas threw them back onto the region as sand, beginning about 1700 million years ago. These sediments now form the Arnhem Land Plateau and probably also the sandstone that crops out in the Mount Tolmer plateau of Litchfield National Park, and other plateaux south and west of Darwin.

Top of Tolmer Falls, Litchfield National Park

Tolmer Falls, Litchfield National Park

Kakadu escarpment

A remarkably long stable interval followed, from about 1650 to 150 million years ago, during which the rocks, which we know as Australia, had drifted at least half way around the world, from the north pole to the south pole. During all this time the extraordinarily resistant Arnhem Land sandstone has operated as an effective cap-rock, protecting and preserving the mineral rich deposits beneath.

The sandstone plateaux eroded from their edges and where they have eroded, they have exposed portions of the ancient Proterozoic landscape. These have persisted with surprisingly little modification to form significant elements of the landscape today, such as the hills we see as

we drive south down the Stuart Highway towards Katherine, and east along the Arnhem Highway towards Kakadu National Park. The road cuttings through hills on these routes nearly all reveal rocks that are older than 2,000 million years which were deposited in the ancient rift-valley.

At about 150 million years ago the region was fringed by fresh water lakes, lagoons and estuaries, and about 115 million years ago, during the Cretaceous, the sea flooded the region from the north-west. At this time much of Australia lay within a warmer Antarctic circle. Northern Australia lay at about the latitude of Tasmania today. The flat-lying, young Cretaceous sediments are deposited on top of the steeply dipping ancient rocks of the Pine Creek Geosyncline. Often enough, rocks of startlingly different ages sit like this, on top of one another. The gap in between indicates that the region has been land and exposed to erosion. Geologists call this an "unconformity". The boundary between the Cretaceous sediments and the rocks of the Pine Creek Geosyncline is one of the most extraordinary unconformities that exist in the world today, since it represents a gap of some 1,700 million years.

The unconformity is well-exposed in the cliff faces of the south-west part of the Shoal Bay Peninsula and on the southern fringes of the Cox Peninsula.

The sea retreated to the north-west about 110 million years ago, and exposed the sedimentary rocks to a long period of erosion. These rocks form the main, present day features in Darwin. The thickness of the Cretaceous rock varies from 2 metres at Doctor's Gully to 40 metres at Lee Point. Various units of this rock, known by geologists as the Darwin Member of the Bathurst Island Group of rocks, can be recognised in several places, particularly at Bullocky Point.

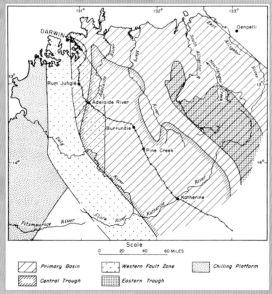
Diagram 1: Map showing Geosyncline through Pine Creek.

Darwin Member rock, East Point.

Porcellanite

Some of the old buildings in Darwin such as the former Palmerston Town Hall and Infirmary are built from porcellanite. This rock is actually the claystone/siltstone unit of the Cretaceous-aged Darwin Member rocks, which are exposed along the cliffs around Darwin. Porcellanite, in particular, has been impregnated with silica-rich groundwater which has hardened and strengthened the otherwise weak claystone.

Porcellanite, Nightcliff Beach

Porcellanite, foreground with laterite and layered conglomerates on laterite in the background, Nightcliff Beach

Casts of belemnites, probably Dimitobelus sp. No internal structure is present in the casts, their composition appears to be identical to the phosphatic nodules lying adjacent to them.

The lowest layer is conglomerate with granule to cobble-sized grains, derived from the ancient rock beneath. Next comes a brown-coloured sandstone which has a greenish tinge when freshly exposed. On top of this is the main unit of the Darwin Member, a fine-grained claystone and silty claystone. Exposures of this unit can be up to 30 metres thick and are invariably colourful and mottled, due to selective leaching and redeposition of iron oxides. The Darwin Member contains interesting fossils, including those of "sea monsters" such as Ichthyosaurs and Plesiosaurs, over 110 million years old (see pg 14-16).

The claystone of the Darwin Member is also rich in fossils of radiolarians. Radiolarians are single-celled, marine planktonic animals which are rarely preserved in sediments because their silicon skeletons are usually dissolved. Belemnite casts are also common in the claystone. Belemnites were marine molluscs, related to today's squids and octopuses.

The Dripstone Caves area at Casuarina Coastal Reserve has massive beds of the Darwin Member. These rocks contain fossils of a disorderly array of worm tubes. These "bioturbated" layers (churned-up sediment resulting from the activity of animals) are not more than 30 cm thick and are interbedded with similarly thick layers of rock containing nodules and pellets of a rock type known as phosphorite, which is possibly derived from the fossiliferous layers. Bioturbated beds are best developed in the claystone on eastern Cox Peninsula where the beds are several metres thick and contain abundant burrows up to 60 cm in length and 1.5 cm in diameter.

Inside Dripstone Caves, Casuarina Coastal Reserve

After the Cretaceous sea drained away to the north-west, a long period of intense chemical weathering followed. This has led to what is known as laterisation. Here, the fabric of the original rock is obliterated and replaced by weathered material cemented together by iron oxide and silica. Laterites are common in the Top End and, because they are often tougher than the parent rock, cap many of the hills and cliffs. The cliffs around Darwin are capped in places by laterite. Good examples can be seen at Dudley Point, East Point Reserve.

A period of uplift about 15 million years ago resulted in rejuvenated erosion. Rivers, laden with sediment, debouched from the plateaux and dissected foothills, dumping sediment in alluvial fans. In time these fans coalesced to form a broad apron which slopes gently northward. This is known as the Koolpinyah surface - the gently rolling, forest-covered landscape (other than the coastal plains) that surrounds Darwin.

Woodland up to laterite cliffs of Warruwi (Goulburn Island)

One interesting feature of the Koolpinyah landscape is the presence of numerous closed depressions, which form the little billabongs sprinkled around Darwin. Some of these billabongs are aligned, and seem to represent buried, old river systems. Others occur apparently at random and their origin is a mystery. Whatever their origin, today they are of considerable importance to the animal life during the long dry season.

Howard Swamp

Here, in leafy, warm Darwin, it is hard to believe that we live in an ice-age. The present ice age is characterised by regular glacials, punctuated by short interglacials (one of which we are currently in). Because we are human, and live in the present, we tend to view today's climate as the norm. Nothing, however, could be further from the truth.

The last time conditions were like they are today was 125,000 years ago, during the last short inter-glacial.

We are, ourselves, ice-age animals, which have evolved during the past 2.5 million years during which there have been 25 recognisable glacial-interglacial cycles. During these cycles, the great continental ice sheets of the northern hemisphere and Antarctica wax and wane, in turn locking-up and releasing water, resulting in world sea levels rising and falling through 150 metres. The last time of very low sea level was 20,000 years ago, when much of Australia was colder, drier - with about half as much rainfall - and windier than today. Australia, New Guinea and Tasmania formed a single land mass and the northern coastline was 400 km to the north of the Top End as Diagram 2 shows.

As the ice sheets melted and sea levels rose, the prehistoric inhabitants of northern Australia were forced relentlessly inland. The melting of the ice-caps resulted in an average horizontal loss of land to the sea of around one metre per week! Imagine this: at a rate of 1 metre per week on Australia's northern shore the social and ecological effects would have been dramatic, perhaps even disastrous in some ways.

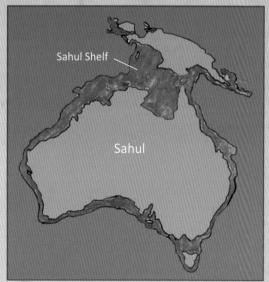

Diagram 2: Map of Australia, New Guinea and Tasmania 20,000 years ago.

It was an incursion that even short-lived human beings would notice! Camps on the hind-dunes and beach fronts would have to be abandoned monthly, lines of dead trees would have marked the new edge of the encroaching sea, inland populations would have had to deal with new invaders forced from their homelands. Mangrove coasts would have been destroyed, eliminating important food sources, reefs and sea-grass beds would have disappeared "out to sea", wiping out important fishing grounds.

Shoal Bay coastal plains, looking towards Palmerston

Dripstone Cliffs, Casuarina Beach

The land bridge between Australia and New Guinea was severed by 9,000 years ago, and by 6,000 years ago the sea had reached its present level, although it was actually further inland than it is now, resulting in what is known as a "big swamp" phase. Our coastal plains are, in fact, younger than 6,000 or 7,000 years. Mangroves soon trapped the sediment washed down from rivers, burying the big swamp, raising the level of the land and pushing the sea back. Even today, a dam cannot be dug more than about two metres deep on the coastal plain because of the reaction of oxygen with the anaerobic mud which forms acidic soils, which can leach toxic metals from the soil and cause fish kills.

By 4,000 years ago, meandering tidal rivers traversed this newly formed, flat coastal plain in large sinuous loops. By 2,000 years ago many of the loops pinched closed and detached from the parent river, forming lagoons and other wetlands. The rivers became less sinuous, and for reasons not completely clear, less of an impediment to salt water which once again tended to flow back onto the plains. Looked at in this way, salt water incursion - today seen as one of the largest environmental problems of the region - is in reality only the result of inexorable long term processes, as the land and the sea seek to strike an equilibrium with each other.

Dudley Point, East Point

One of the intriguing geomorphological features on the coastal plains in the Darwin region is the result of the slowly growing coast line. Roughly parallel to the shoreline but converging towards the various headlands is a series of low, narrow ridges or "beaches" built of shelly sand and studded with Pandanus palms. They are called "cheniers" and often result from infrequent catastrophic storms which smash shells and hurl them into mounds to form a beach. In front of the chenier ridge the mangrove belt once again advances slowly seaward. Behind the chenier ridges, sedges eventually colonise the now protected mud-flats, raising the surface of the land until the flats emerge above tidal limits.

Chenier ridges have been dated in various places in the Top End, and vary from 4,490 years old to 670 years old. Cameron Beach has the best developed chenier plain in the area and radio-carbon ages there indicate a rapid growth of the chenier plain seaward since 2350 years ago - the age of the hindmost ridges. While Cameron Beach constitutes the best chenier plain, you can see chenier ridges on most beaches which are open to the sea. Mindil Beach, Coconut Grove and Casuarina Beach all have chenier ridges. Chenier ridges and coastal plains are the youngest and most dynamic features in an otherwise ancient landscape where the tempo of change is much slower.

Chenier ridge edging beach and coastal plain

Darwin's "Sea Monsters" from the Cretaceous

Ichthyosaur, illustration

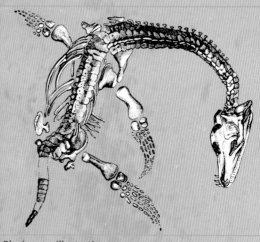

Plesiosaur, illustration

In Darwin, it is not so much Jurassic Park, as Cretaceous Park. On the geological time scale the Jurassic and Cretaceous are next to each other, with the Cretaceous being the younger. About 110 million years ago, in the Cretaceous, the area around Darwin was washed by a gentle, shallow sea in which swam reptilian ichthyosaurs: in fact the word is a compound from ancient Greek, meaning "fish" and "lizard".

Ichthyosaurs were reptiles, shaped like sharks but with long, dolphin-like snouts. From their gut contents we know that they ate fish, now-extinct belemnites (a little like squids), and squids. All these are fast and agile - ichthyosaurs must have been an agile and fast swimmers. They grew to about seven metres.

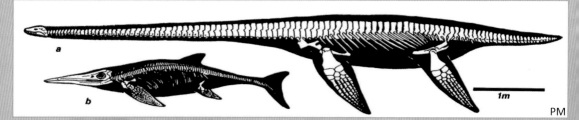

Scale restorations of Darwin Area plesiosaur and ichthyosaur, based on sizes of representative fragments:
a, Elasmosauridae *gen. et sp. indet*, **b,** *Platypterygius sp.*

At least three localities around the cliffs of Darwin contain fossils of ichthyosaurs. Unfortunately, while the fossils are relatively common, they are not well preserved. In fact, the rather daunting scientific name of the Darwin animal, Platypterygius gen. et sp. indet., simply means that scientists are not yet sure of the exact identity of the animal, hence it is 'indeterminate'. Fragments of the Darwin ichthyosaur have so far been found in rock outcrops near Nightcliff, Casuarina and Fannie Bay. The exact location of the Fannie Bay ichthyosaur has not been documented, since the chunk of rock containing it was removed in the early part of this century.

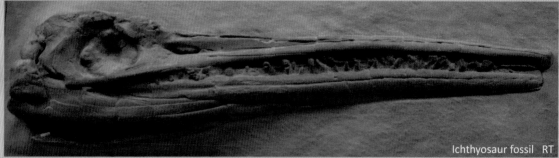

Ichthyosaur fossil RT

At Nightcliff, the fossils are found in a thin (4 – 6 cm) bed of fossiliferous shaly siltstone which is overlain by 20-30 cm of reddish brown, lateritised, fine sandstone. At Casuarina, the outcrop is exposed only during spring tides. The top of the siltstone 'reef' containing the ichthyosaur fragments can be seen, projecting less than one metre above the adjacent and surrounding sandy beach.

People looking for Ichthyosaurus fossils, Nightcliff foreshore.

Isolated adult ichthyosaur dorsal vertebral-centra consisting of silicified bone. - Nightcliff

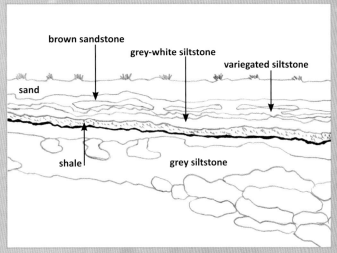

Diagram 3. Cross section of Nightcliff foreshore.

This outcrop also has embedded in it fossil bones of a plesiosaur, another marine reptile, much larger than the ichthyosaur. The relative size of the ichthyosaur and plesiosaur are indicated in the diagram adjacent. Access to the locality is by road to the "Casuarina Free Beach". Most of the fossils are of vertebrae or casts of vertebrae. The ichthyosaur fossils are often associated with fossils of invertebrates such as molluscs and belemnites, and, in Casuarina, of fossilised wood.

The fossilised wood is a bit of a mystery. Palaeontologists have pondered on the idea that carcasses of ichthyosaurs, like drift-wood, ended up stranded along the Cretaceous sea shoreline, which, around Darwin, was in a similar position to the coastline of today. Because of the nature of Darwin's ichthyosaur fossils - the fact that they were deposited in an active marine environment (as opposed to a deep ocean), and the fact that carcasses of today's marine animals, such as seals and whales, can float for weeks without disintegrating - palaeontologists believe that the Darwin region may have been an area where dead ichthyosaurs from more distant regions ended up.

Ichthyosaur fossil, Nightcliff

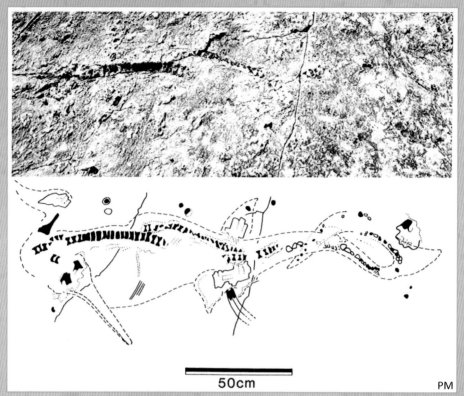

50cm

PM

Ichthyosaur fossil, Nightcliff with diagram

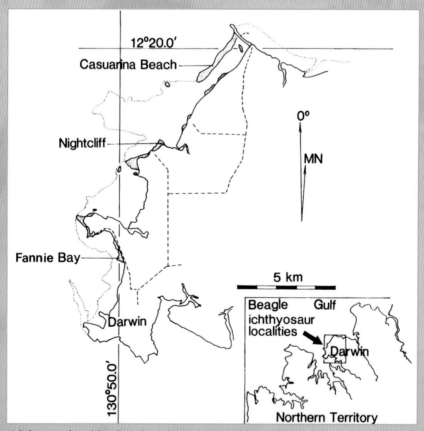

Ichthyosaur locatities, Darwin region

The Ever-changing Shoreline

The soft sedimentary cliffs of Ansen Bay, near the mouth of the Daly River, face the monsoonal gales each year during the Bärra (north-west monsoon).

This feature is a common sight along the Top End coastline and the rapid rate of erosion seen here is countered by sedimentary deposition in quieter inshore waters such as bays and esturaries. In these situations we see the development of extensive tidal forests.

CHAPTER TWO

The shaping of the environment; the Biogeography of the Top End

The northern Australian tropics are characterised by a belt of Eucalypt-dominated open forest and woodland extending from the Kimberley, across the Top End, along the Gulf of Carpentaria and into eastern Queensland. Within this leafy framework are small, moist pockets left over from the past when Australia lay in high latitudes, first as part of a wetter Gondwana and then as an island continent drifting north from about 50 million years ago to its present latitude.

From about 15 million years ago, Australia began to dry out. In the Top End, the year-round wet climate shifted to a seasonal climate with a pronounced dry season. The vast expanse of lowland, temperate rainforest, which extended from northern Australia to southern New Guinea (the mountains had not yet formed) in a vast, level plain, began to shrink.

Monsoon forests, adapted to seasonal conditions, were already well established in the tropical lands to the north of Australia. They harboured species that were widespread and dispersed readily. These supertramps began to establish themselves in northern Australia by floating in on mats of vegetation, by being carried by fruit-eating birds and bats, who spread their wings to welcome the new big southern neighbour, or by being blown in. Stowing away on the floating mats of vegetation was the occasional Asian migrant. The ancestors of the Top End's magnificent tree rats and rock rats arrived this way, as did some reptiles, now well and truly integrated into poly-ancestral Australia.

While most of northern Australia's monsoon forests have affinities with Asia, some species, like the Arnhem Land escarpment species *Allosyncarpia ternata*, are relicts of the old Gondwanan temperate rainforest that was shrinking, retreating to refuge areas in north-east and east Australia. Its parting gesture was the eucalypt-based flora that now forms the matrix of the wet/dry tropics of the Top End.

Eucalypt forest evolved on the fringes of the temperate rainforest around the time that the first globe-trotting monsoon forest species began hitch-hiking to Australia. By the Pleistocene, 2 million years ago, monsoon forests had moved in to stay, and formed a mosaic with the contracting temperate rainforest and the still small patches of dry sclerophyll forests.

Grand *Allosyncarpia ternata*

Allosyncarpia ternata forests cluster in patches through the escarpment country of Kakadu and Western Arnhem Land

Rats as big as cats – Djintamoonga and Koorrawal

The Top End is home to two of the largest rats in Australia, the Tree-rats. Djintamoonga, the Black-footed Tree-rat *Mesembriomys gouldii* and Koorrawal, the Golden-backed Tree-rat *Mesembriomys macrurus* frequent the woodlands and forests of the region, climbing trees adeptly and living in the hollows. Koorrawal, the Wunambal Aboriginal name for this beautiful animal, is now rare in the region, found most commonly in the north-west Kimberleys. It was recently sighted in Kakadu National Park, the first time since 1969.

Djintamoonga, the Tiwi Aboriginal name for this powerful and spectacular animal, grows to about 290 millimetres, plus a tail of over 350 millimetres, tipped with white bristly fur. Its feet, ear tips and tail are black, and the pelage is grey-black. It is relatively common in some areas, and can be seen occasionally in open forest by spotlight. Both Tree-rats eat a variety of fruits, plants and insects.

Golden-backed Tree-rat *Mesembriomys macrurus*

Black-footed Tree-rat *Mesembriomys gouldii*

As large as these changes appear to be (since Australia drifted into seasonal climates) they were almost nothing compared to the onslaught of the climatic oscillations of the current ice-age (see Chapter 1). Conditions can be guessed at by noting the changes that occurred in one rainforest patch in the Atherton Tableland of north Queensland during the last interglacial-glacial-interglacial cycle. Here, good pollen records show that a rich tropical rainforest of flowering plants withered 50,000 years ago to become a cooler conifer-dominated rainforest. As the region entered the glacial peak of 18,000 years ago, rainforests were entirely obliterated, to be replaced by a sclerophyll forest dominated by Eucalyptus and Casuarina. Only 10,000 years ago, as the climate ameliorated into that of the current inter-glacial, did the rich flowering forest return. And this was only one of 25 such cycles that have occurred in the last 2.5 million years!

In the Top End this climatic see-sawing has resulted in the total withdrawal of the temperate rainforests that dominated Australia for tens of millions of years. Seizing its chance, the Eucalypt-based forest expanded. The monsoon forests, however, were having an identity crisis. During the glacial maxima they clung on in small local refuges or disappeared entirely. During the short, punctuated interglacial periods, like today, they tentatively expanded. Today, the monsoon rainforests of northern Australia occupy a total area of about 2750 km², fragmented into about 16,000 patches, none of which is greater than about 30km². In addition these are now separated from the wet tropics by shallow seas and arid hinterlands. What we see today, then, is a shadow of a former glory.

How did animals cope with this sort of treatment? Interestingly, this is the sort of stuff that evolution is made of. Australian birds, mammals and reptiles rose to the challenge and evolved into forms, which could successfully occupy these new forests. The ecological echoes of these relatively recent events, however, still reverberate strongly through time to affect the structure of present-day animal communities.

The Red-winged Parrot, for instance, is thought to have evolved from ancestral stocks, represented today by the Australian King-Parrot that inhabited primal rainforest pockets and now rainforest and tall wet forest on the east coast of Australia. The Red-winged Parrot, which is widespread in the Top End, differentiated from the ancestral parrots at the drier boundaries of the rainforest, finally shunning the rainforest altogether, to spread into the eucalypt-covered hinterland.

Red-winged Parrot

The Silver-crowned Friarbird, a noisy, cackling, common Top End bird, evolved from the Helmeted Friarbird which occupies moist forests throughout northern Australia, New Guinea and the Lesser Sundas of Indonesia. During the Pleistocene glaciations, the Helmeted Friarbirds fell back to moist refuges in Cape York, southern New Guinea, protected gorges along the Arnhem Land escarpment and patches of forest in the Kimberley. Severe aridity, particularly in the Kimberley, forced the Helmeted Friarbird to adapt to change leading to the evolution of another species, the Silver-crowned Friarbird, which emerged to successfully occupy the drier forests right across the Top End.

Silver-crowned Friarbird

In the meantime, the impenetrable (for some birds) arid hinterlands of the Gulf of Carpentaria meant that the Helmeted Friarbirds in Arnhem Land were never able to regain contact with their own species on the east coast. Further changes here caused this population to split into two, one retreating to an isolated population within the Arnhem Land escarpment, and the other occupying mangrove and coastal monsoon forest.

It is easy to see how this might have come about, if it is realised that the coastline (with its mangroves and monsoon pockets) would have been much further north during the last glacial period. This would have separated the two formerly adjacent populations of Helmeted Friarbirds, *Philemon buceroides*, into a coastal population, *Philemon buceroides gordoni*, and an escarpment population, *Philemon buceroides ammitophila*. Too long apart, by the time they came together again in today's environment, the differences were too great for mingling.

The Banded Fruit-dove, the White-throated Grasswren and the Chestnut-quilled Rock-Pigeon are birds that became totally restricted to the refuge area of the Arnhem Land escarpment during the Pleistocene glacials. Today, they are only found on the escarpment.

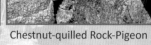

Banded Fruit-dove   White-throated Grasswren   Chestnut-quilled Rock-Pigeon

Monsoon Forest at Territory Wildlife Park

Other rainforest and monsoon forest birds took to the only other closed-canopy forest - the mangrove communities. In comparison to the dizzying evolutionary see-sawing going on in the monsoon forests, these were stable. As a result of this and the fact that the Top End is probably the evolutionary centre for mangroves, we have the most distinctive mangrove avifauna in the world (pg 25).

The Top End's rich bird fauna, however, is richest in the Eucalypt forests. Because the forests are so widespread the avifauna is also generally widely distributed in northern Australia and more than 90% of the species occur either in Cape York or the Kimberley in addition to the Top End.

While it is not surprising that the monsoon forests have a depauperate bird fauna, a significant component of birds, and some bat species too, do prefer them over savanna vegetation. This difference reflects the greater dispersal ability of birds and bats. Unlike lizards and land mammals, they can fly over tracts of largely inhospitable landscape to exploit small rich patches. The same birds and bats probably also found refuge in mangrove habitats during periods when monsoon rainforests largely vanished from the landscape.

This option was largely unavailable to most herpetofauna that are unable to move quickly over large distances. Only three species of reptiles and amphibians occur exclusively in monsoon forests. These are the Dark-tailed Skink, *Sphenomorphus nigricaudis*, and MacFarlane's Skink, *Carlia macfarlani*, and also a frog, *Rana daemeli* In the Northern Territory, these species are restricted to monsoon forests in eastern Arnhem Land and Melville and Bathurst Island. They are probably the only Top End remnants of a specialised rainforest herpetofauna. The rest of the fauna either disappeared or evolved to occupy other habitats when the rainforests disappeared during the arid periods of the Pleistocene.

MacFarlane's Skink - *Carlia macfarlani*

Rana daemeli

Mammals in the Rainforest

Northern Brown Bandicoot - *Isoodon macrourus*   Grassland Melomys - *Melomys burtoni*

Not surprisingly, the lack of a rich distinctive monsoon rainforest avifauna and herpetofauna is paralleled in terrestrial mammals. There are no distinct mammal fauna closely associated with monsoon forest in the Northern Territory. Many of the rainforest specialist mammals retreated with the temperate rainforests to the extensive rainforests of the Wet Tropics of north-east Australia. Here a rich and distinctive mammal fauna is a mirror to what much of northern Australia looked like 15 million years ago. There are, however, some species of mammals here in the Top End that, while not specialists on rainforest, do favour them. Interestingly, these same species also occur in Cape York but only as generalist species or as species characteristic of small and degraded rainforests, for example the Loolong or Grassland Melomys, *Melomys burtoni*, and the Northern Brown Bandicoot, *Isoodon macrourus*.

The drastic changes in sea level during the Pleistocene glaciations have also had an impact on the marine environment. For instance, at the peak of the two most recent glaciations approximately 18,000 and 135,000 years ago, the sea level dropped to such an extent that the entire area between New Guinea and Australia formed an expansive plain, with not a Barramundi in sight. Only at the very warmest periods, 7,000 years ago to the present, and previously from 130,000 to 115,000 years ago, were sea levels of a height sufficient to open the shallow 7.5 metre deep Torres Strait. The populations of Barramundi reflect these changes. Genetic studies have shown that the differences that exist between the populations on the east coast of Australia and the Top End populations are due to the populations being separate for 108,000 years (from 115,000 years ago to 7,000 years ago).

Mangrove Reptiles

Whereas mangrove birds became isolated, which lead them to diversify, mangrove reptiles in the Top End were in most cases, strongly linked to populations in Cape York, New Guinea and SE Asia. The widespread Mangrove Monitor *Varanus indicus* and Bockadam *Cerberus australis* are good examples of this. Being confined to the thin and very mobile strip of habitat between land and sea where mangrove communities develop, the major fluctuations in sea levels over time would have forced serious and constant geographical movement for these populations.

Mangrove Monitor - *Varanus indicus*   Bockadam - *Cerberus australis*

Birds of the Mangroves

Rufous Night Heron - *Nycticorax caledonicus*   Great-billed Heron - *Ardea sumatrana*

Probably all mangrove-dependent species of birds in Australia have arisen from rainforest-inhabiting ancestors. The story of how this came about highlights the impact that rising and falling sea levels have had on the Top End's flora and fauna and explains the paradox of why the Top End, with fewer species of mangrove plants, have more mangrove birds than the wet tropics, richer in mangroves.

As Australia cooled and dried, particularly over the past two million years, New Guinea and Cape York served as refuges for the formerly widespread rainforest birds. The close proximity of rainforest to mangroves meant a constant interchange amongst bird populations and hence there was no isolation to force birds to speciate in mangroves.

The situation on the Arafura Land plain was quite the opposite. Here, the dry climate, west of the Great Dividing Range, supported open forest at best. Rainforest birds fled to the mangroves which themselves were patchy and isolated. This process offered great opportunities for speciation and the evolution of the most distinctive mangrove avifauna in the world.

Chestnut Rail - *Eulabeornis castaneoventris*

CHAPTER THREE

The Torrid Lands; The Climate of the Top End

Darwin is a dazzling city in a land of never-ending warmth and light. Situated at the centre of the wet/dry tropics, the Top End is consistently the warmest region of Australia, where hours of light differ by no more than 1.5 hours throughout the year. These comfortable, though somewhat humid, conditions make living in Darwin a little like living in a warm, secure womb. The maximum day-time temperatures at Darwin rarely vary much from 32°C and minimum temperatures, overnight, from 19°C to 25°C.

27

From a plant's perspective, however, life is lived more dangerously. This is because Darwin's rainfall is seasonal, on average 1650 mm spread over 4-7 months. Nowhere else in Australia is this seasonality so reliable. We can guarantee half a year of drought, and a flood - every year. This savage alteration of soil moisture each year can be likened to living in a rainforest for part of the year and a desert for another, with mad oscillations from deluge to drought in the in-between period. These extreme oscillations are because the rain falls in intense storms with permanently high, tropical levels of evaporation in between.

The climate of the Top End and Darwin is "monsoonal", an evocative term that is usually associated with India and southeast Asia. In fact, "monsoon" simply means "seasonal wind", and these affect large areas of the planet both north and south of the equator.

On Earth, atmospheric winds sweep from the high-pressure systems in mid-latitudes (where cool air is descending, causing pressures to increase) to a belt of low pressure which girdles the planet (where warm air is rising hence decreasing the pressure). This belt is known as the inter-tropical convergence zone, or monsoon trough, and it tracks the latitude of highest surface temperature. This latitude varies with the inclination of the sun, and is found, for instance, in the northern hemisphere in July, and in the southern hemisphere in January, slicing across the Top End. The region of the equator itself is relatively calm.

In general, during the dry months between May and September, the wind sweeps across the Australian continent from the southeast on its way to the monsoon trough, north of the equator. Darwin and the Top End are in the path of these relatively cool, dry continental winds and hence receive perfect, blue-sky weather at this time (see diagram 4 pg 36).

As the sun moves south of the equator, to position itself over northern Australia between November and February, intense surface heating occurs and a thermal low pressure system forms over northern Australia. This thermal low pressure system, helped by the push from strong north easterly winds from high pressure systems over Siberia and northern China, drags winds in from the north, across equatorial waters and pulls the monsoon trough south. The moist, warm, air rises, becoming very unstable and forming spectacular anvil-shaped clouds, looking like vast, snow clad mountains in the sky.

This process is assisted by winds converging from the southeast. From October to December, while the monsoon trough moves toward Australia's northern coastline, the Arnhem Land escarpment helps catalyse the uplift of this unstable but dryer air, which forms the spectacular thunderheads of the build-up. These clouds drift like battalions toward Darwin, throwing out spears of lightning and cannon-like thunder, and only occasionally relieving the charged atmosphere with cooling rain.

Darwin is the lightning capital of the world as a result of this phenomenon, and scientists from around the world are currently studying the process to work out why Darwin is so electrifying. Build-up cloud also forms on the air boundary where the more or less northerly afternoon sea-breeze collides with the prevailing wind (usually easterly at this time of the year). Build-up clouds dissipate out to sea.

The monsoon trough migrates south, moving over Darwin generally from December to March. In some respects the term "The Wet" is a little misleading since the Top End and Darwin do not receive one continuous monsoon burst, but rather several bursts. The average first monsoon burst in Darwin arrives in late December.

While each year brings a drought and a flood, the strength and duration of the flood varies considerably. The Top End's "Big Wets" are becoming famous through television documentaries and stories, but they do not happen every year. Interestingly, the events that influence the strength and duration of our wet seasons are played out thousands of kilometres away in the east Pacific, off South America.

Normally cold water from Antarctica rises to the surface along the west coast of South America coast. This water extends northward as the Humboldt current, eventually flowing westward along the equator where it is heated by the tropical sun. The result of this cold current is that the east Pacific is cooler than the west Pacific and a circulation pattern known as the Walker circulation is established, shown in diagram 5 (pg 36). Here, the air over the relatively cooler water descends in a high-pressure system. At the surface this air moves, as the easterly trade-winds to the low pressure system over the Indonesian region. Here it rises and moves in the upper levels toward the high-pressure system where it once more descends. When this circulation is strong - that is with strong trade-winds and warmer sea temperatures to the north of the Top End - the chances are that northern Australia will have a strong monsoon trough, penetrating deep into the Australian continent and causing a "big wet".

During what is known as El Nino years, on average every four or five years, the opposite situation occurs. During these years a warm ocean current develops off the west coast of South America, in the vicinity of Ecuador and Peru. This current usually makes its appearance around Christmas time, hence the name El Nino, which translates to 'the boy-child' and refers to the Christ child. Under the influence of the El Nino current the eastern Pacific may be as warm as the western Pacific. The Walker circulation then weakens as slackened trade winds feed less moisture into the Indonesian region. During El Nino years there is a high probability that eastern and northern Australia will be drier than normal. The monsoons will likely arrive late and be weak.

The reason we have lightning at all, is because of the basic and remarkable nature of water, H_2O. Essentially, it is composed of two positively charged hydrogen atoms, and one negatively charged oxygen atom, which, together, form a stable, neutral marriage. The bonds are not strong, though, and the atoms can regroup into one positively charged hydrogen ion and a negatively charged hydroxyl ion (one hydrogen atom and one oxygen atom). The other remarkable thing about water is that it expands when it freezes. If it didn't, ice would be heavier than water, sink to the bottom of the sea, and very quickly freeze the whole planet by stopping ocean currents from turning over and warming up.

Lightning forms in cumulonimbus clouds, where raindrops freeze. For reasons which we are not yet certain, the electrons within a freezing raindrop migrate, causing it to become charged, or ionised. Raindrops freeze from the outside-in so that, eventually, the expansion of freezing water inside the already frozen skin bursts the ice into splinters which are charged positive or negative. Perhaps because the positive ions are lighter (only one hydrogen atom), they are funnelled to the top of the cloud in the updraughts. The negatively charged area at the bottom of the cloud further induces a positive charge on the ground. This follows the cloud like a shadow, just as magnetised bits of iron follow a magnet along

Air, particularly dry air (like the south-easterlies rising over the escarpment), is a poor conductor causing enormous electrical potentials to build up. Finally, when the differences between ground and atmospheric electrical charge are enough (several hundred million volts) to overcome the insulating effect of air, a stream of electrons bursts towards the ground, travelling at 100 km per second, in 50 to 100 metre steps, seeking the path of least resistance. This "stepped leader" is usually invisible to the naked eye, but when it touches the ground a return stroke flashes upward along the ionised path that the leader has created. Then it is on for one and all, and an avalanche of electrons pulsates to the ground in multiple lightning strokes - as many as 42 each lasting thousandths of a second. An average thunderstorm can release several hundred megawatts of electrical power, probably enough to power a small town in each storm.

About 30% of lightning strikes actually strike the ground, and they strike where the positive charge is greatest, such as trees, tall buildings and particularly metal towers and rods. The old saying that lightning does not strike the same place twice is false - just ask a lightning conductor

Lightning heats the air along its path to around 30,000°C, nearly five times the surface temperature of the sun, causing rapid explosive expansion of the air. Cooling is equally rapid. The result is that the air is shaken violently, generating a shock-wave, which we hear as booming thunder. A feature of thunder is that it is bent upward by the faster rate of travel within the lower warmer air, so that thunder cannot be heard beyond about 20 km. The distance away of lightning can be judged from the time between the flash and the bang since sound takes about 3 seconds for each kilometre of travel through the air.

People struck by lightning can be hurled several metres by the shock-wave. They may also find that they have been relieved of their clothing. This is because the sudden expansion of air inside their garments may blow the garments off.

Safety Tips for Lightning

Lightning kills. But the chances are far less than being killed in a car accident. There is no risk to people inside a steel-framed building, a metal aeroplane or an enclosed vehicle. Do not use phones during storms, and turn off and unplug modems and computers (for the computers' sakes). Anyone caught outside in a storm should stay away from external walls, chimneys, metal pipework or electrical wiring such as TV antenna wires. What ever you do, do not hold aloft an umbrella, golf club or fishing rod. Outdoors you should avoid the edges of forests, isolated trees, tents or sheds, power lines and masts, swimming pools, metal fencing, mountain edges and open spaces. (It does not leave much, does it?)

- If you cannot take shelter, avoid elevated places and crouch down and keep your head as low as possible but do not lie down as a surface current from lightning may travel through your body and cause harm.

- If your hair begins to stand on end and your skin begins to tingle and you hear clicking sounds, it is time to move away.

- People struck by lightning are usually rendered unconscious and can stop breathing. Cardiopulmonary resuscitation is essential.

A key to the clouds of the Top End

From the silky filaments of high altitude cirrus to the towering, awesome mass of cumulo-nimbus, clouds are fascinating. Who cannot remember gazing at them with wonder as they shape-shift across the sky, here a dragon, there a galleon?

Clouds are the visual evidence of the presence of water in the atmosphere. As moist air rises it encounters lower pressures, expands and cools. Water vapour then condenses into tiny droplets to form a cloud. About one million cloud droplets are contained in one rain-drop. Clouds are white. It is only when viewed from the ground that some appear shades of grey, deeper clouds forming darker shade, or because clouds are shaded from higher cloud.

There are 10 main cloud types, which are further divided into 27 sub-types according to height, shape, colour and associated weather. Clouds are categorised according to the height of their base above the ground; low clouds have bases from the Earth's surface to 2.5km; middle, with bases from 2.5km to 6.0km; or high, with bases above 6km from the earth's surface. A cumulonimbus cloud which may extend up to say 18 kilometres is still classified as 'low' because its base is typically only about 500-600 metres above the ground. Below are the common cloud types seen in the Top End, grouped according to the times that certain clouds are most likely to be seen:

Latin names are used in the classification of clouds.

cirrus means a hair
JB

stratus means layer
DL

cumulus means a heap

Dry Season

During the dry months, warm air rises from the hot ground to produce heaped cumulus cloud. The trade-winds from the south-east flatten out the top of these clouds to produce strato-cumulus cloud. This is the most common cloud type of the dry season.

The same type of cloud occurring at mid-level is called altocumulus.

Upper level cirrus clouds indicate the movement of larger weather systems across the continent. They are filaments of cloud made up of ice crystals.

Build-up Months

During the build-up months the winds shift direction and begin to come from the north and north-west. The humidity increases and cumulus cloud forms. Showers of rain may occur.

Cumulus cloud which grows unimpeded forms rising mounds, domes and tower cumulus cloud. The sunlit parts of these clouds are brilliant white; their bases are dark and nearly horizontal.

As the tower cumulus continues to grow it forms a mountainous cloud which can be up to 16 km high. These are the Top End and Darwin's famous cumulonimbus clouds. From a distance, the upper portion can appear as an anvil or plume. This is caused by strong upper level winds spreading out the colder ice crystals. Lightning and thunder are characteristic of this type of cloud.

Monsoon

As the monsoon trough, or inter-tropical convergence zone, approaches from the north, lines of thunderstorms develop. The air, after these lines pass over, is still dense with water vapour and often forms a blanket of middle-level altostratus cloud.

During the monsoon itself the air is thick with moisture - virtually an ocean in the sky. Here, blankets of low and mid-level stratus and alto-stratus cloud, in which cumulus and cumulonimbus clouds are embedded, loom over Darwin and the Top End.

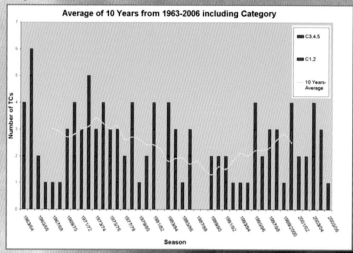

Average of 10 Years from 1963-2006 including Category

C3,4,5

C1,2

10 Years-
Average

Number of TCs

Season

Cyclones

Tropical cyclones - often referred to in the northern hemisphere as hurricanes or typhoons - are intense low-pressure systems forming over seas at low latitudes, with spiraling wind speeds exceeding 63km/hr surrounding the centre. Severe tropical cyclones have surface wind speeds in excess of 120km/hr surrounding the centre and have been known to bring up to 1140 mm of rainfall in 24 hours.

The suction of the rapid swirl around the centre pulls air down from high in the atmosphere causing a calm, dry eye. Eye diameters are typically 40 km but they can range from under 10 km to over 100 km. Outside the cloudless eye there is a raging vortex of damp air ascending from the warm ocean, with tall clouds about 15 km high forming a wall. Wind speeds and rainfall are greatest here.

Tropical cyclones are energised by the accumulation of latent heat as warm air evaporates from warm oceans. They do not form unless the sea-surface temperature is above 26.5°C. The up-draught of unstable air causes extreme low pressures which in effect drag air in from the surrounding higher pressure areas. As the air rushes in, it is deflected by the spin of the Earth (known as the Coriolis effect) to create a clockwise swirl in the southern hemisphere (the other way in the northern hemisphere). The air accelerates as it moves into a tighter rotation, just as skaters spin faster when they draw their arms in.

A tropical cyclone takes an erratic track affected by many factors, including nearby high-pressure systems, the proximity of land and the upper winds. Once on land, the tropical cyclone usually decays inland as a result of the dry surface and the friction of the land's roughness. The time from detection of a tropical cyclone to its disappearance varies between a few hours and three weeks, but is normally about six days.

Ironically, tropical cyclones can be seen as safety valves since they export the energy, as latent-heat, to higher latitudes, through upper-level outflow from the vortex.

Tropical cyclones can form only between about 5° and 20° north and south latitude (though once formed they can maintain their identity well poleward). Nearer the equator, the Coriolis effect is too small to start the rotation, while at higher latitudes the ocean surfaces are too cool.

A Queensland Government Meteorologist, named Clement Wragge, started giving personal names to individual cyclones. This predilection caused strong objections from politicians whose names he used: they protested about being linked with disasters! Wragge then changed to feminine names. In these emancipated days, tropical cyclones are given either male or female names and are named according to an internationally adopted sequence.

Tropical cyclones devastated Darwin in 1882, 1897 1917, 1937 and again in 1974, when Cyclone Tracy hit the city. Since Tracy, Darwin has been affected by more cyclones, which produced minimal damage. Categories of cyclone severity range from 1 for a cyclone just reaching cyclone strength to 5 for the most severe. Some examples of cyclones falling within each of these categories is found in the graph on page 34.

Cyclones occur on an average of 7.7 days per season in the Darwin region (the Bureau of Meteorology's northern region). Of the 46 cyclones recorded in the northern region since 1970, 35 were relatively weak (category 1 or 2 cyclones). Most of the cyclones in the Darwin region are small in size. Tracy, for instance, while nasty, had gale force winds extending only 40 km from the cyclone centre. Joan, in Western Australia, on the other hand, had gale-force winds extending to 170 km from the cyclone centre.

The Bureau of Meteorology is responsible for detecting, tracking and issuing warnings of tropical cyclones. The Darwin office is equipped with sophisticated communications equipment and special facilities to enable quick responses to the changing threat posed by a moving tropical cyclone. The Bureau is an excellent source of information about tropical cyclones and other meteorological phenomena, which affect Darwin and the Top End.

JB

January

July

Position of ITCZ — Near-surface streamlines

Diagram 4

Walker Circulation

Trade Winds

Warm pool

Water heated by the Sun

New Guinea

Upwelling

South America

Thermocline

Cool lower water

Diagram 5

WInd devastion from Cyclone Monica in western Arnhem Land, 2006

JRS

CHAPTER FOUR

Natural rhythms;
natural history of the Top End
according to seasons

In a womb-warm climate dominated by monsoonal rain, spring, summer, autumn and winter are alien concepts. Non-Aboriginal residents usually talk about 'The Wet', 'The Dry' and 'The Build-up'. Aboriginal people, in contrast, recognise seasons according to the rich and complex behaviour of animals and plants and the characteristic sights, sounds and smells of the season.

Gun-djehmi Calendar

Andjalen the Woollybutt starts to flower

Yamidj the Green Katydid calls out that the cheeky yams are ready

Anbedje, Spear Grass knocked down by storms from the SE

Everything flooded, Start of Dunbug, egg time (Magpie Goose)

Anrebel the Stringybarks begin to flower

The Best Fruit Trees, Andudjmi, Green Plum, Andak, Yellow Plum, Andjarduk, Red Apple, An.gundalk, Black Plum, Start to flower.

Anboiberre, White Apple in flower

Andjalbbirdu, Pink Apple in flower

Anmarriwahwah Leichhardt Tree

© Morris, 1978 adapted from seasonal calendar of N.E.Arnhem Land

Anboiberre, White Apple now fruiting

Kakadu Region

Aboriginal people in the Kakadu region recognise six seasons, which are generally applicable across the Top End. The calendar above shows the names of these seasons in Gun-djehmi (Mayali) language as well as some of the more obvious natural phenomena that occur in these seasons, such as the wind changes that indicate seasonal changes, we have combined the cool seasons into one.

The spectacular seasonality of the Top End has resulted in a number of equally spectacular seasonal adaptations. Using these, it would be possible to tell which season you were in, even if you did not have a calendar. So that coming to the Top End or Darwin at any time of the year promises some fascinating phenomena. Keep an eye out for them when you arrive to explore the city and its surrounds. Where possible, we have focused on plants and animals, which are described in the field guide section of Part Two under the appropriate habitat section.

View of Darwin city from Wagait Beach

Pre-Monsoon Storm Season - Late October to Mid December

A good place to start, the early rains of a new life-replenishing wet season begin in October-November. Non-Aboriginal people call it the 'build-up'; a time of high heat and high humidity when people tend to 'go troppo'. The tension in the air is reflected in the electrifying thunderstorms that produce little rain (see Chapter 3).

For Aboriginal people, this is the time to hunt and collect yams, fruits, fish, File-snakes, Flying Foxes, and Saltwater Crocodile eggs.

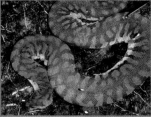

Arafura File Snake

The favourite long yams fatten during the rainy season and are ready to dig after the leaves have yellowed

Red Apple

Black Flying Foxes

For the wildlife itself this is the period of great excitement and activity. Cicadas herald the approaching wet season, yams and orchids put out new leaves, blue-tongue lizards and frilled lizards appear from their hiding places, the latter flaunting their expanded frill to intimidate other males and attract females. Fully grown male Barramundi move down the rivers and into the estuaries.

Northern Blue-tongue Lizard

Barramundi, TWP

Cicada

Frilled Lizard

Magpie Geese

In the Top End, the Northern Green Tree Frog uses any hollow pipes, hollow branches, washing machines and toilets as sound shells from which to resonate. Magpie Geese wing their way in graceful columns across the evening sky to newly available food. Pheasant Coucals find their summer voice to boom their presence.

Green Tree-frog, *Litoria caerulea*

New leaves of *Allosyncarpia ternata*

New leaves of *Terminalia ferdinandiana*

The forests surrounding Darwin, and right across the Top End begin to fill-out as new leaves appear on the many deciduous and semi-deciduous trees. The deciduous nature of the forests of the wet/dry tropics is unique in Australia. Even the Eucalypts, which elsewhere are evergreen, here drop up to 50 per cent of their leaves. In fact, the bigger the leaves the more deciduous the tree. In a place where a seasonal drought is guaranteed, this adaptation has allowed the forests to conserve water and cope with the long dry season. What is incredible is that the new shoots appear before the first rains, so that they get a head start on the awakening, ravenous insects.

Ants and termites, however, are not fooled and they begin to swarm before the first storms, getting their large, organised nests ready to release the winged reproductives with the first rains.

Also arriving in flocks before the first storms is the Little Curlew (opposite page). The Little Curlew is just one of the many migratory waders that arrive in Darwin from the river valleys of the tundra, northern Siberia, either to stay or just passing through on the way further south. Most of these international visitors arrive in the hot, late dry season. There is also some exodus, and the Straw-necked Ibis, Glossy Ibis, Black Kites and Bee-eaters leave for the less torrid climate of southern Australia.

Termite alates take flight

Shorter distance inter-continental migrants, which migrate to Australia for the wet season are the Common Koel, the Dollarbird and the Torresian Imperial Pigeon. Each of these species breeds in and around Darwin and the Top End and then, except for some Torresian Imperial Pigeons which choose to reside in the Top End, moves back to New Guinea and surrounding islands during the dry season.

Common Koel or Rainbird

Dollarbird

Torresian Imperial Pigeon

The Common Koel or Rainbird is locally known as the 'brain-fever-bird' because of its unendearing habit of shrieking in ever rising tones to a frantic climax. This can go on all day (and half the night). Thankfully, only the male is so brain-fevered as the female is relatively quiet. The female Koel, like most cuckoos, lays its eggs in other birds' nests. She prefers species like friar-birds and orioles and times her laying to coincide with theirs.

The Dollarbird notes its return from New Guinea with harsh 'kak-kak-kak' calls and aerial displays where it shows-off its distinctive white circles on the underside of the wings - the so-called 'dollars'.

The first Green Plums appear. The small green fruits that have large stones surrounded by a thin layer of sweet flesh, are not quite ripe during this season. Other bushtucker, which appears includes the native peanuts of the Red-fruited Kurrajong or Peanut Tree.

Green Plum, *Buchanania obovata*　　　　JB　　Peanut Tree, *Sterculia quadrifida*

Little Curlew

Perhaps the best known migrant among the locals of Darwin is the Little Curlew. These birds arrive in mid-September from their breeding grounds in central and north-eastern Siberia. On route, they fly along the

east coast of China, and through Japan, the Philippines and Sulawesi. Then, almost the entire world's population flies on to Australia, funnelling through Darwin and nearby coastal plains on the journey south.

Walking and flying through the streets of Darwin, they are as numerous as the tourists.

They congregate, sometimes in their thousands, not on the beaches and reefs, like their fellow Siberian travellers, but on the dry subcoastal plains and on ovals and suburban lawns where they pick and probe in the cracks in the soil, taking seeds, caterpillars and other invertebrates.

To the locals, the bird heralds the beginning of the wet season. Yet, when the wet season comes the birds flock together to escape the flooded ovals and plains and move inland, staying on dry ground.

Little Curlew

Wet Season – Mid December to March

Spear grass, *Sorghum intrans*

Spear grass, *Sorghum intrans*

Perhaps the greatest spectacle of this season is the growth, flowering, seeding and withering of the sorghum (spear-grass), each stage painting the landscape a subtle new colour. By December young sorghum sprouts are already obvious in the woodlands and alongside the roads, looking as if they have been deliberately planted. As the season progresses, the plants elongate casting a pale to mid-green hue across the landscape. This gradually changes to salmon-pink, which quickly deepens as the sorghum develops rust-coloured streaks. Clouds of pale pollen puff out when the grass is disturbed. Then for a few days the chocolate coloured seed-heads paint the landscape deep rust. This, however, is not a good time for walking about in the tall towering grass, which grows well above head height since the mature seeds spear and then twist aggressively into clothing and skin. Most of the seeds fall to the ground where they twist into the soil to wait until the next wet season.

Cricket

Katydid

Pheasant Coucal

Yellow Oriole at nest

Young katydid crickets emerge from the ground to grow with the spear grass, which is their food. The crickets grow through several stages and emerge as adults when the spear grass matures and seeds. At this time the cricket sings, heralding the maturation of the spear grass. It is a noise that local Aboriginal people recognise as the katydids saying, 'the yams are ready to dig'. Zzzzzzzzzzzzzzzzzzzzzzzzzzzt, Zzzzzzzzzzzzzzzzzzzzzt.

Rainbow Pitta

Along with the katydids, the staccato calls of cicadas and the honking, plonking and ringing sound of breeding frogs creates an unforgettable, deafening, soundscape which leaves a buzzing in the ears even when the katydids are not singing.

The Pheasant Coucal is now in full voice. Its booming 'coop-coop-coop' descends and accelerates as it displays to any female who pays attention. Many birds breed during this time of plenty. In the monsoon forest patches, the pretty Yellow Oriole and beautiful Rainbow Pittas are nesting.

Insect-eating birds are more likely to breed at the beginning of the wet season in response to the increase in insect numbers. Frugivores, granivores and waterbirds, in tune with their various ripening resources, breed a little later than these. Pink-eared Duck and Hardhead can turn up in Darwin during December.

Pink-eared Ducks

Reef Egrets

Waterbirds, in particular, breed mostly in the late wet season, when water levels have stabilised and when aquatic vegetation, invertebrates and fish have reached maximum abundance.

The Long-necked Turtle, which has been entombed beneath cement-like clay for the entire dry season, tapping into its reservoir of body fat, finds its prison dissolving, and emerges ravenous. Many species of frogs are also released from their entombment by the first rains. The largest of them, the Northern Burrowing Frog, hones-in on other calling frogs and devours them.

Northern Long-necked Turtle

It is worthwhile taking a closer look at the wetter, swampier, low lying places. Out of the dry season, fire-blackened and heat hardened infertile soils will appear, like magic, beautiful and delicate flowers such as trigger plants, bladderworts, sundews and orchids. Some of these delicate flowers have indelicate habits and, perhaps because of the infertility of the soil, extract extra nutrients directly from animals. The tiny carnivorous bladderworts, for instance, have special traps, triggered by hairs that suck in unsuspecting insects. The pretty sundew arranges its leaves in a little rosette. Glands on the leaves secrete glistening, sweet-looking syrup, which is really an adhesive - nature's super-glue. The glue holds down and digests any insect that has blundered onto the leaves.

Stylidium sp.

Utricularia fulva

Drosera sp.

Nervilia plicata

Rain fills the swamps, creeks and billabongs and gushes downstream. Tiny fish - new hatchlings - appear in schools struggling upstream. They fight their way into shallow grasslands and swampy areas. Sometimes they even swim up gutters and end up on flooded lawns. The Rainbow fishes are commonly seen in creeks at this time of the year. They grow to about 110 mm. Ants, native rodents and snakes are forced from flood-prone underground homes, sometimes into people's homes.

A rich sweet smell issues from watercourses and local billabongs where the paperbark trees are flowering. Billy Goat Plums, *Terminalia ferdinandiana*, perhaps the richest source known for vitamin C are abundantly available on the low sprawling trees in the Eucalypt forests. Aboriginal people sometimes knew the monsoon season as the hard season. Much of the land is underwater, the rivers are flowing high and strong, and the wildlife is spread out across the country. Most yams are flooded, but fish, yellow spotted monitor, water pythons, snapping turtles and magpie Goose eggs are in abundance.

Chequered Rainbowfish

Yellow-spotted Monitor

Northern Snapping Turtle

Water Python

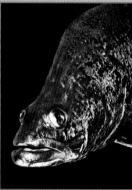
Barramundi

A woodland in the rain, and the bright green spear grass grows

The Late Storm Season – March to April

Known locally as the 'knock-em-down' storm season, this short season, centred on April, is characterised by localised storms and strong winds. Apart from cyclones these are the strongest winds of the year and arrive from the south-east. Barramundi use these last flushes of water to swim upstream to their dry-season billabong homes. The storms knock down (hence 'knock-em-downs') large patches of sorghum, which quickly cures to a pale straw colour. The first fires of the on-coming dry occur now, but they rapidly go out.

Knock-em-down storm

Speargrass knocked down by the storms

Black Kite

These fires are the cues for the return of the Black Kite, which arrive from central Australia, heralding their return with their characteristic whinnying call. They thrive on the insects and reptiles, which flee fire. The numbers of Sacred Kingfishers also rise sharply in March and April, and then decrease just as suddenly, suggesting a passage through Darwin to Indonesia where they are quite common. Also look out for the Red-headed Honeyeater. Normally confined to mangroves, the Red-headed comes into suburban gardens due to the lack of flowering in the mangroves at this time.

Pools of water, now fully stocked with tadpoles, are still sprinkled across the landscape. They are adorned with blue waterlilies, *Nymphaea violacea*, which also provide feeding sites for young Magpie Geese. Agile Wallabies feed on the green grasses edging the wetlands.

DL
Speargrass fire

Worming into your socks, clothes and into any defended or undefended body crevices, seeds are a reminder that the bush (and you) are alive and newly invigorated by the wet season. Native seeds often work like guided missiles and are designed to ensure that they become buried deep within the soil to escape the dry season fires, and reappear as seedlings after the first rains of next season. About 10 percent of the seeds actually produced are required to replace the parents. The rest becomes food for a variety of animals, whose lifestyles are organised around the excess. Ants are perhaps the most important of these animals and as much as 90 per cent of certain seeds can be harvested by them. They leave conspicuous piles of seed husks around the entrances of their nests. Keep an eye out for finches, such as the Double-barred Finch, for which seeds are also a bonanza.

Ants carrying grass seeds to their nest

Yams are again available for food, fish and wallabies are to be caught, goannas are abundant and fat, and Magpie Goose eggs are still to be found.

Carnivorous flowering plants in black soil

Northern Nail-tail Wallaby *Onychogalea unguifera*

47

Cool Seasons - May - July

By now the wet season has well and truly disappeared over the northern horizon with the monsoon trough. Along the roadsides, the bush brightens with splashes of yellow-flowering Acacia and red-flowering Grevillea, and their fragrant scents waft on the cooler, drier air. Saltwater Crocodiles need to bask in the sun in the morning to warm up, and local human Top-Enders may be seen wearing a jumper, even though the temperature may be 25°C!

Acacia dimidiata

The cooler season provides a wide range of food for traditional Aboriginal people. Goannas will be less plentiful shortly, and snapping turtles are reaching the end of their season as food, but yams, fish, and many other foods are abundant. Flying-foxes become much more abundant, much to the relish of the local gourmands. Later in the cool dry season, in some areas, Freshwater Crocodiles lay their eggs, mussels become more abundant, and File-snakes and Magpie Geese are once again included in the varied seasonal menu.

Grevillea goodii

Rainbow Bee-eaters

Saltwater Crocodile basking in the sun

Rufous Whistler

The penetrating trill of the Rainbow Bee-eater announces the return of many birds from southern latitudes. Some birds may not come from very far south at all. For instance, Black-faced Cuckoo Shrikes whose numbers increase rapidly during the dry in Darwin, are known to breed in the wet season just south of Darwin, at Batchelor. While Rufous Whistlers are seen in the mangroves through the majority of the year, the White-winged Trillers are not often in Darwin during the wet season. Nevertheless, they are found between Pine Creek and Katherine, about 200 km or so south.

Black Flying Fox

Other species that arrive in the Top End during the dry season, or whose numbers swell to many times that of the wet season include the Tree Martin, White-breasted Woodswallow, Olive-backed Oriole, Magpie Lark, Red-tailed Black Cockatoo, Red-backed Kingfisher and the Australian Pratincole.

Red-tailed Black Cockatoo

White-breasted Woodswallows

One of the most impressive local migrations involves the Banded Honeyeater. This little tyrant typically overwhelms other species in numbers in its quest for flowering eucalypts and melaleucas. Virtually unseen in the wet season in Darwin, it is quite nomadic and is often seen south of Pine Creek. The Varied Lorikeet is another bird that is highly nomadic, appearing often in high densities in Darwin during the dry season.

Chestnut-breasted Mannikins

The grasslands and sedgelands of the drying floodplains, too, are occupied by a substantial number of birds, some of them resident and others migrants in the dry season. Where vegetation is dense, the small Golden-headed Cisticola and the Chestnut-breasted Mannikin may be resident. Less dense grassy areas harbour species that have returned from the inland such as the Australian Pratincole.

As floodplain waters recede during the dry season, a number of non-breeding waterfowl from southern Australia can be found in the Top End's wetlands. Prominent are Grey Teal and Purple Swamphen. These are nomadic species adapted to seeking out any available shallow, freshwater swamps throughout the continent. Also look out for the not commonly seen Spotted Harrier, which is seeking out favoured areas in the northern part of its inland range.

In contrast to nearly all other bird groups, which breed in and around the wet season, raptors (birds of prey) breed in the dry season. From a raptor's point of view this certainly makes sense because at this time the ground cover is sparser and prey - particularly young, immature prey - are at a maximum, making hunting an easier task.

Purple Swamphen

Kapok Bush, *Cochlospermum fraseri*   Turkey Bush, *Calytrix exstipulata*   Woollybutt. *Eucalyptus miniata*

In the forests the trees are once again beginning to lose their leaves. Some trees are already completely deciduous such as the Kapok Bush which also flowers at this time, an unmistakable bright yellow flower. The purple-pink of the Turkey Bush is also an unmistakable sign that the dry season is here. One of the dominant eucalypts, the Darwin Woollybutt is flowering now. The beautiful orange blooms can be seen in its still-leafy canopy.

Turkey Bush and Kapok bush in the foreground with Fern-leaved Grevillea behind

Barking Owls perched in a Casuarina   Boobook Owl

Hot Dry Season – August to October

From August to September, temperature and humidity once again increase. This season is characterised by dust, smoke and haze, and incredible sunsets. Fires burn hot (see page 54), attracting clouds of raptors, mainly Black Kites and Brown Falcons, which hunt small, fleeing animals. As if in celebration of fire, cycads produce sprays of bright green that provide a stunning contrast to the scorched black earth. The cycads then set seed in time for the wet season. Orchids and lilies often flower first, using the energy stored in their root-stock during the wet season, so that their seeds will also be ready for the

Cycas armstrongii, new leaves   *Cycas armstrongii,* female fruits

wet. In fact, rather than risking desiccation, many plants have their energy stored safe-and-sound in bulbs under the ground. The apparent lifelessness of the forest floor at this time is merely an illusion. Up in the canopy, however, leaves are hanging-on limply, waiting for the life-giving rains.

In the meantime, Freshwater Crocodiles are laying eggs in the sandy creek banks. And, at night, the bush is alive with the sounds of breeding owls, both the 'wuff-wuff' of the Barking Owl and the 'more-pork' of the Boobook Owl (see opposite page).

But before the rains it is the migratory waders from Siberia that sprinkle onto our floodplains and tidal flats. Approximately 60 species of birds migrate to the southern hemisphere during the boreal winter, our summer. Darwin is one of the 20 most important sites for aggregations of waders within Australia. It is the closest of these sites to south-east Asia and the archipelago of Indonesia. Approximately 30 species are seen regularly. Long-distance migrant species generally arrive in Darwin during September, but maximum numbers are in either September or October, boosting the number of Top End birds. Few of them are resident in Australia.

At times there can be significant numbers of Curlew Sandpipers, Red Knot, Bar-tailed Godwit and Red-necked Stints on the coast and in the fresh-water wetlands, Sharp-tailed Sandpipers, but these tend to pass through on their way south. Many species, however, such as the Great Knot, Black-tailed Godwit and Greater Sandplover remain in the north, far outnumbering those that continue further south. The Common, Greenshank and Marsh Sandpiper are more likely to be the most common species over the complete season, which extends into the build-up.

Bombax ceiba flowers

In September, a major flowering sequence begins in riparian forests beginning with the Silver-leafed paperbark trees, Melaleuca argentea, followed by Broad-leafed paperbarks, *Melaleuca viridiflora* and Weeping Paperbarks, *Melaleuca leucadendra*. This flowering attracts high numbers of different honeyeaters including the Brown Honeyeater, the Rufous-banded Honeyeater and the Bar-breasted Honeyeater. On river levees and in monsoon forests, large red flowers adorn the deciduous Kapok tree, *Bombax ceiba*. In the woodlands, the large globular fruits of the Pandanus, *Pandanus spiralis*, turn from green to orange-red. The magnificent orange flowers of the Silky Grevillea, *Grevillea pteridifolia*, drip with nectar and along with honeyeaters, attract lorikeets and cockatoos. White, downy fibres of native kapok tumble from the seed-pods of the Kapok Bush.

This is the season for the many yams, fish, Freshwater Crocodile eggs, file-snakes, magpie geese, flying-foxes and wallabies. Long-necked Turtles appear once again in the campfire pits.

Kapok seed pod, *Cochlospermum fraseri*

Mouse Spider

The Darwin Mouse Spider, is common in and around Darwin, often found wandering through gardens or inside buildings in the build-up and early wet season when the males are out prowling for a mate. Mouse spiders are about the size of a 20 cent coin. They are black with a light grey to white patch on the back of their bodies. The head is wide, shiny and black with eyes spread across the front. They are often confused with Funnel-web Spiders whose bite can cause severe illness or even death in humans. Funnel-webs, however, have not been found in Darwin. The Mouse Spider does strike readily and can inflict a painful bite, though not as serious as the Funnel-web's bite.

Mouse Spider *Missulena pruinosa*

Another spider, not so commonly encountered, is the Barking Spider. This large, powerful and hairy spider has a body length of up to 6 cm and can be various shades of brown ranging through grey. Few humans have been bitten by the Barking Spiders. Those that have been bitten have symptoms, which include inflammation, intense discomfort at the site of the bite, nausea, vomiting, headaches and fever. While the spider does not actually bark, it does produce a whistling sound by rubbing together its mouth parts - sounding like crickets and grasshoppers.

Barking or Whistling Spider *Selenocosmia sp.*

Sugar Bag

In the past, Aboriginal Top-enders relied heavily on bush honey (sugarbag) as their only source of fast energy. Today, sugarbag is still a favoured food, and the best time to go searching for sugarbag is in June or July when the stringybark flowers appear. There are 1600 diminutive native bee species in Australia, quietly going about the business of pollinating native flowers. Strongly individualistic, most of these species work alone. Five species of native bees, however, work communally and also produce honey. In the Top End, the most common is *Trigona hockingsi*. They are small and black and do not sting. Unlike most of the rest of the native bees, Trigona lives in colonies and collects pollen and nectar to produce honey, which is dark and strong. The nests are found inside termite mounds, tree trunks and branches and even in buildings. Dark, waxy, tell tale marks, give away the small entrance to the nest. Nests consist of a cavity lining, a cluster of brood cells, and honey and pollen storage pots.

Trigona sp. at tree hive

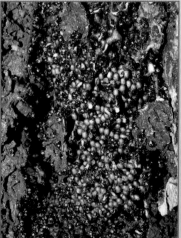

Bees and pollen inside hive

Trigona sp. with pots of honey

Brown Honeyeater

The Brown Honeyeater becomes locally common around Darwin at the end of the wet season. At this time, in March or April, it will mostly be flitting about open woodland where Eucalypts such as *E. porecta* are flowering. A regular succession of eucalypts and other trees such as *Grevillea pteridifolia* and *Xanthostemon paradoxus* continues to produce nectar in woodlands until late August. In and around Darwin, the Brown Honeyeater also utilises mangroves during the dry season. In

Brown Honey-eater in *Xanthostemon*

Brown Honey-eater on nest

September a flowering sequence begins in riparian forests, beginning with Silver-leafed Paperbarks, Melaleuca argentea, drawing in Brown Honeyeaters like a magnet. Densities of other honeyeaters also become high in this spatially restricted habitat at this time. As soon as the Silver-leafed Paperbarks cease flowering, the Brown Honeyeaters move on to other flowering aggregations of melaleucas. At the end of the wet season, Brown Honeyeaters begin returning to the woodlands and open forests once more.

The Weighty Wetlands

Where in the world is the highest tonnage of wildlife found? The Serengeti plains of Africa? Or the plains of South Africa perhaps? The correct answer is the Adelaide River floodplain 60 kilometres south-east of Darwin. Here, at Fogg Dam, is a writhing mass of water python estimated to have a biomass of up to 1.0 tonnes per square kilometre. The reason for such an extraordinary water python weigh-in is the equally extraordinary numbers of the native Marrawata or Dusky Rat, *Rattus colletti*, which thrives here on the rich floodplain vegetation. During the day, a trip to Fogg Dam is a birder's delight. But at night water pythons in their thousands mobilise from their daytime reedbed refuge to hunt for the rats which emerge from the cracked sun-baked soil. If you visit Fogg Dam during the dry season in the evening, an hour or two after sunset, you can almost be guaranteed of seeing a python.

Water birds at Fogg Dam

Smoke haze and savanna fires

Billowing columns of smoke and a hazy atmosphere often greet visitors to Darwin and the Top End during the dry. It may seem as if you were visiting a landscape on fire. In many respects this is true since fire has been a natural part of the tropical savanna for at least 15 million years. In pre-human times, fires would have been ignited by lightning. Aboriginal people modified the fire regime when they first arrived perhaps 50,000-60,000 years ago, influencing and largely molding the composition of flora and fauna of the wet-

dry tropics. Here, as elsewhere, they burned patches of country throughout the year so as to reduce the negative effects of uncontrolled wildfire.

Traditionally, also, Aboriginal people burnt patches of country at different times of the year to stimulate this flowering and fruiting so that fruit was available over a longer period of time. Some of the most common grasses, such as sorghum (speargrass) can be managed by timing burns before seed sets in the early dry season. In this way other grasses and plants can get a hold and grow for a season. In some areas, fires are lit early in the dry season to protect buried turtles from being killed later in the year by hot fires.

Example of a cool, early burn, where there is still leaf litter.

Today, fires are lit by pastoralists, Aboriginal and non-Aboriginal land managers and park managers. In some areas Aboriginal people use fire to manage their traditional estates, for a range of hunting, gathering and cultural responsibility purposes. Aboriginal people and Park managers light fires in the early dry season to protect important plant and animal communities such as the monsoon forests and creek lines, and some of the special waterholes and swamps from the hot destructive fires of the late dry season. Graziers light them to open up the country for cattle and game to feed on the new shoots. Some fires are lit to provide fire-breaks to protect forest, woodland and pasture from the ravages of hot season wildfires.

Example of a late season burn, which causes devastation to life in the forest.

Top End plants and animals exhibit many responses to fires. If you have the opportunity to see a fire burning, watch for the frenzy of activity around the leading edge. Park well away from the fire, so you are not a danger to others, and sit and observe. Hundreds of Black Kites and Whistling Kites and sometimes Little Eagles and others can be seen swooping to the ground. They are chasing the animals fleeing the fire - the grasshoppers, rats, mice, marsupials, small birds, lizards, snakes and beetles which form a major part of the diet of these aerial hunters.

Even though the flames leap high this is still a cool afternoon fire

Smoke cloud over Fogg Dam

Magpie Geese

An unusual bird, the Magpie Goose is neither magpie nor goose. Biochemical studies have shown that the Magpie Goose is in fact most closely related to screamers, (family Anhimidae) of South America. The relationship is not that close (and besides, Magpie Geese honk) and, as a result, Magpie Geese have been elevated to a family of their own, the Anseranatidae. One of the oddities of the Magpie Goose, enabling it to exploit a range of resources, is its feet. While they are weakly webbed, to allow the bird to swim and dive, there is also a long unwebbed portion of the toes including an opposable fourth toe.

Geese congregating in the wild rice, *Oryza rufipogon*

This very un-goose like characteristic allows Magpie Geese to clamber through thick swamp vegetation, grasp and manipulate grass stems for nest building, and perch - rather clumsily - in trees, away from predators.

This range of behavioural adaptation also allows it to tap into the changing nature of resources in the Top End. At the end of the dry season, Magpie Geese move to the swamps and billabongs that still contain water, and await the arrival of the wet season rains. At this time they feed by grazing on the blades of grasses that grow on the edges of swamps. In fact up to 70 per cent of the Magpie Goose diet can be grass blades at this time.

The early rains in November and December trigger enlargement and development of the sex organs, which is complete in January in both males and females. By this time, the swamps have filled, from the monsoon rains, and Magpie Geese begin to gather where there is a reasonable growth of spike rushes or thick grass in water up to two metres deep. The Magpie Geese bend and trample the spike-rushes and grass stems, and weave them into platforms. The platform is shaped into walls around a deep cup just before the birds begin to lay. Laying may begin as early as January and as late as May, depending on the season, the depth of water, and the availability of food for adults. Most breeding takes place in the late wet season when the water levels are stable and the vegetation in the swamps is at a peak.

The eggs take about four weeks to hatch, and the goslings fledge in ten weeks. By now, the aquatic grasses such as wild rice *Oryza rufipogon* have produced abundant seeds, and both adults and juveniles are able to feast on the seeds without having to travel too far. More than 80 per cent of their diet are seeds at this time.

The goslings fledge as the dry season progresses. Magpie Goose families may then seek out deeper swamps where grasses may still be seeding, but mostly they dig up the bulbs of the spike rushes on the drying swamps which contain water to about 30 centimetres deep. Bulbs dominate the diet from the middle of the dry season. In their search for this food, Magpie Geese gather in huge mobs on extensive monospecific stands of spike-rushes known locally as 'goose camps'. The largest of these 'water chestnut' swamps occur in Kakadu, and these can attract hundreds of thousands, perhaps even millions of Magpie Geese from many parts of the Top End. When the Magpie Geese have exhausted this food supply or the ground is baked to a hard pan with the bulbs trapped within, the birds move back to the perennial swamps and billabongs and begin eating grass blades again.

Goose digging for bulbs of spike-rush, *Eleocharis dulcis*

Seasonal movement is a way of life for Magpie Geese. No single locality is occupied by the birds throughout the year; rather, the different resources available at different localities are used in a seasonal progression. In this way, Magpie Geese are similar to most species of waterbirds; just the details of their movements and the resources they select are different.

Magpie Goose at nest with chicks and eggs

The Bird Nectar Calendar

As Australian as marsupials, our honeyeaters evolved from ancient Gondwanan ancestors. Despite the name, Australian honey-eaters also eat insects, which is not surprising given Australia's abundant insect resources. To obtain the relatively sparsely-spread nectar, even sedentary honey-eaters must travel, at least locally. The extent of migration by woodland honeyeaters varies significantly and depends on the proximity of their "nectar habitats".

Through much of the Top End, including Darwin, Katherine, Kakadu, Litchfield, Daly River regions the bird calendar goes something like this:

In January and February (the wet season), the Broad-leafed Paperbarks, *Melaleuca viridiflora*, surrounding local billabongs are flowering profusely, attracting any species of nectarivore within smelling distance. This is followed or overlapped by Weeping Paperbark, *Melaleuca leucadendra*, and paperbark, *Melaleuca cajaputi*, the latter of which occurs both along watercourses and along the margins of mangroves. Other important nectar sources toward the end of the wet season include the shrubby *Grevillea decurrens*, the prostrate *Grevillea dryandri* and various mistletoes.

By the beginning of May (the dry season), most coastal paperbarks have dried up, and *Eucalyptus polycarpa* and *Eucalyptus bleeseri* take over. By June or July the Woollybutt, *Eucalyptus miniata* and its close relative *Eucalyptus phoenicea*, in rocky areas, are in flower, providing a feast for a whole suite of birds, not restricted to nectarivores. Look out for insectivorous trillers to frugivorous orioles, granivorous Northern Rosellas and carnivorous butcherbirds. Fern-leaved Grevillea, *Grevillea pteridifolia* offers rich rewards for the larger honeyeaters and lorikeets, while *Banksia dentata*, where it occurs, is popular mainly among smaller honeyeaters. Closer to permanent rivers, Silverleaf Paperbark, *Melaleuca argentea*, may be the main draw card (see also Brown Honeyeater pg53).

There are few large flowerers in the late dry season apart from the White Gum *Eucalyptus papuana*. Other plants flowering include *Eucalyptus clavigera*, *Terminalia grandiflora*, *Lophostemon lactifluus*, *Planchonia careya*, *Brachychiton paradoxus*, and near watercourses, *Melaleuca dealbata*.

In November and December, the early wet season, a new suite of plants is flowering, notably *Xanthostemon paradoxus*, a crooked evergreen tree, related to the eucalypts, which is extremely popular with all nectarivores. This is followed once again by the paperbarks.

Dusky Honey-eater in *Grevillea dryandri*

Magnetic Termite Mounds

South and west of Darwin a debris-feeding termite called *Amitermes meriodionalis* constructs remarkable termite mounds in clusters of 20-100 in seasonally-flooded, low-lying flats. Like tombstones all in a row, the long axes of the mounds are aligned north-south. Unique to Australia, only one other related termite, *Amitermes laurensis*, builds meridional mounds like these.

Scientists testing the orientation of the mounds have discovered that the orientation of the mound has little to do with magnetism but a lot to do with minimising temperature variation inside the mound. The mounds are oriented so that they are warmed rapidly in the morning due to the heating of the eastern face. In the noon-day sun only the thinnest profile of the mound is offered. In the evening the mound's western face is warmed by the setting sun.

The reason the exacting termites go to such trouble is because their mounds are subject to seasonal flooding, which does not permit the termites to escape underground. For the soft, white, heat-sensitive bodies of termites it is crucial that the above-ground refuge be thermoregulated.

Interesting, when you come to measure the exact orientation of the mounds at different sites, you find that the mounds are not all oriented the same. Cleverly it seems that the termites at individual sites adjust the exact orientation of the cluster of mounds to fit with even micro-environmental scale variation such as amount of shade, orientation to the cooling winds, and surface temperatures, so that the optimum orientation for individual sites is selected.

The Dry Season Dividend

The storm season starts with a great expectancy. It is as if every life form knows what is coming. Suddenly, animals that have been inactive for months, spring to life and then begin the search for high-energy food, which will allow them to compete for mates with other members of their species. The vital fuel is provided from a most unlikely source - termites!

All dry season, the numerous varieties of termites, some grass harvesters, some wood recyclers and some litter removalists, have been busy doing a job that no other member of the ecosystem can do - recycling cellulose and on a massive scale. To do this, the many known species construct large storehouses, above or below ground, and this allows them to work on through the year, even if fire sweeps through and robs them of their seasonal resources.

Coptotermes at mound / nest

Part of the success of these communal insects is in the way they live. Whether in majestic mounds or hollow trees or below ground, their extensive galleries and storehouses are temperature, light and humidity controlled. Each species adapts its architecture to the specific habitat and some varieties, like the famous Magnetic Termite *Amitermes meridionalis*, which live on seasonally flooded plains, concentrate their living to 'high-tech cooling towers' above ground. The occupants only emerge, generally under the cover of darkness, to harvest or breed when all of those outside conditions are favourable.

In order to reproduce at the end of the dry season, each termite colony prepares a vast number of large, winged, reproductive members called 'alates'. Their job is to fly, on command, 'en masse', up into the atmosphere, find a mate, return to earth as a married couple, shed their 'single-use only' wings, construct a burrow and begin a completely new colony. The colony takes no chances and sends many thousands on a job, which only takes two to complete. Like fighter pilots, they are fed on the best protein-rich foods the colony can produce, ready for that special night.

Carlia longipes with Mastotermes darwiniensis

It appears to be the soldier caste, which determine just which night they will release the alates. They prefer the evenings, just after the first heavy rains when the humidity matches that of the inside of their 'castle'. When the command is given, by the soldiers at the entrance to their tunnel, the alates launch into the atmosphere like smoke out of a chimney. It only takes 10-15 minutes for all the alates to become airborne.

This is the moment that all other life-forms have been watching and waiting for. Tree frogs, spade-foot toads, skinks, dragons, flycatchers, curlews, woodswallows, friarbirds, bandicoots, antechinus, sugar gliders and micro bats - to name but a few.

The idea is to eat as many termite alates as possible while they are available. This quick intake of protein has a remarkable effect on each animal predator and they soon come into breeding condition. This process happens on a massive scale, recharging the whole ecosystem and making it possible for the next vital processes to take place.

The well known Frilled-neck Lizard is a good example. It spends most of the dry season doing very little, usually high in a Stringybark tree, eating the occasional meat ant and avoiding predators. The arrival of the first storm is the signal for all 'Frillies' to descend to the ground and start eating.

Cathedral Termite Mound of *Nasutitermes triodiae*

After feeding heavily on termites in the 'build-up', the male Frilled Lizard is ready to face the challenges of the breeding season

Ants and other invertebrates form the bulk of its intake, but what they are really looking for are signs of the imminent termite flights. Keen eyesight and a quick sprint can have the hungry lizard on the spot at the critical moment. Meanwhile, other lizards and birds move in to mop up the surplus. As this event usually happens after sunset, the night shift quickly arrives to take charge. Curlews, antechinuses and bandicoots are also depending upon the protein intake for their own breeding programs.

It is not just wildlife that benefits from the industry of the termite. Most Eucalypt trees in the tropical woodlands have termite colonies living within their trunks and branches from an early age and contrary to popular belief, the trees benefit from the importation of nutrients. The hollows created by the termites serve as accommodation for many types of birds, animals and reptiles later in the life of the tree. The ground around a termite mound becomes 'nutrient rich' over time as these little, blind relatives of cockroaches work tirelessly to import nutrients from a wide area. Many of these nutrients go into the materials used for the construction of the intricate gallery networks.

Thanks to the ingenuity of the termite, the Aboriginal population of Arnhem Land has been enjoying the sound of the Yidaki (Didjeridoo) long before other forms of man-made music arrived. The hollowing of the young saplings has produced distinctly Australian music.

Termites have certainly played a major role in shaping Australia's savannas. It is thought that this enormous, termite-driven nutrient cycle in Australia is performing the same role as the vast herds of herbivorous animals on the plains of East Africa.

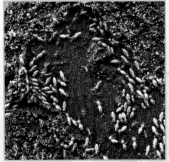

Coptotermes on Ironwood   *Mastotermes darwiniensis*   Launching tower for *Nasutitermes sp.*

A short unnatural history of the Top End

JB

Wild Pig

Compared with the densely populated and highly modified landscapes of Australia's temperate environments, the Top End might seem like one of the last expanses of natural environment left on earth. But the tropical north has, however, been subject to drastic change since European settlement. Invasive and insidious, this change has shredded intricate Indigenous land management patterns and pushed elements of the biota of the Top End into a spiral of decline.

European diseases ravaged Indigenous populations, even before the arrival of Europeans themselves, in the nineteenth century. Pastoralism and mining continued violently to displace Indigenous owners. Their use of fire to progressively build a fine mosaic of burnt and unburnt patches has been replaced with a fire regime that burns up to half the landscape each year in hot, ecologically devastating fires.

Today pastoral leases make up about three quarters of the tropical landscape. Conservation lands in contrast comprise about 6% of the landscape mostly in less fertile areas.

Perhaps surprisingly, given all this, few extinctions have been recorded in the Top End. This is in stark contrast to central Australia which has one the world's highest extinctions rates: 18 native mammals species, about one third of the total desert fauna. That the impacts of European land management have triggered a destabilizing chain of events is, however, now evident in the growing list of endangered animals and plants in the Top End: 14 land mammals, 15 birds, 7 reptiles and a frog, 9 fish, 11 invertebrates and 54 plant species.

The focus of this book unashamedly has been on the vivid natural history of the Top End and Darwin region, but much of what you will find is unnatural. Mimosa, mimosa pigra, forms dense impenetrable thickets in wetlands. Ponded pastures have often replaced native grasses and sedges. Pasture grasses, such as Gamba grass, *Andropogon gayanus*, (see adjacent box) have spread aggressively with irreversible effects on wildlife. Of the thousands of species of pasture introduced because they were considered desirable, less than one percent has likely been of any real pastoral benefit and not become weedy. Not

including cattle, exotic animals, such as cane toads (see adjacent box) buffalo, and pigs are now some of the most obvious and widespread animal species.

Even so, the Top End environments are, to a large extent, intact. Their rugged individuality has shrugged off development ambition that includes wholesale clearing and intensive agriculture. But for how long?

Wild Buffalo

The Cane Toad - How we unraveled the Tropical Ecosystem

The cane toad *Bufo marinus*, is a large toxic toad introduced to Australia by the sugar industry in 1935 from South and Central America to control the native cane beetle. One of the world's most invasive species, there is little evidence that the cane toad had any impact on the beetle. From a population of 101 toads, however, they have now spread across to the top of Australia to the Kimberley. Arriving in the Top End in 2001, they are now the most common vertebrate animal here, eating anything they come across that is small enough to swallow, and laying up to 30,000 eggs twice a year.

Given such a large onslaught, the scientific evidence suggests they have pushed the northern quoll, already in decline, to the brink of extinction. They have also caused reduction in some snake and goanna species. The cane toad is sadly the most recent factor contributing to what is in fact a wholesale shift in land management since European colonization. Changes of fire regime, introduction of feral stock and pastures, and non-native predators and cane toads has now ramified into the wholesale disappearance of mammal fauna from across northern Australia.

There is no known control of cane toads, and in desperation community groups in Darwin have concentrated on 'local control' using mechanical techniques to remove them from small ecosystems, allowing some goannas and the northern quoll to survive in coastal patches.

Cane Toad eating a Keelback Snake   Cane Toad

Gamba Grass

Gamba grass, *Andropogon gayanus*, was first introduced into the Top End of the Northern Territory as a pasture species in the 1930's. Subsequent research and trials resulted in widespread plantings in pastoral and agricultural areas. When heavily grazed, Gamba grass can be a productive and palatable fodder. Unmanaged, Gamba grass has proven to be highly invasive, and is now a declared noxious weed.

Gamba grass grows rapidly to form tussocks that are bigger, taller and denser than native grass species. Whereas grassy fuel loads in native savanna typically approach 5-6 tonnes per hectare, unmanaged Gamba grass infestations can exceed 30 tonnes per hectare—the equivalent of forest fuel loads in southern eucalypt forests.

Fires in Gamba grass fuels can be very intense and effectively unmanagable, especially under windy late dry season conditions. Frequent fires in such infested situations result in substantial loss of the woody overstorey, and almost total replacement of the groundcover. Without any effective means of control, Gamba grass invasion poses a significant threat to regional biodiversity in the Darwin region and potentially in savanna systems across northern Australia.

Gamba Grass

PART TWO:
Field Guide
to the Habitats
of the Top End

CHAPTER FIVE

Woollands and Open Forest

Eucalypt woodlands and open forest are characteristic of northern Australia, extending from the Kimberley to Cape York. These woodlands are typically dominated by two species, Darwin Stringybark *Eucalyptus tetrodonta*, and Darwin Woollybutt *Eucalyptus miniata*. The Stringybark has thick, furrowed bark extending right up to the smallest branches. In contrast, and as the name implies, the Woollybutt's bark covers only the base of the tree, the upper half has smooth, white branches. Ironwood *Erythrophleum chlorostachys* is also widespread and sometimes co-dominant throughout these woodlands.

The understorey layer in eucalypt woodlands varies widely, both seasonally and floristically. Tall grasses are a prominent feature of the ground layer. Native Sorghum or spear grasses are prolific, growing to 4 metres tall and most species complete their vigorous life cycle - from seed germination to seed set - within the span of the wet season.

Many of the understorey trees and shrubs resprout after fire or slashing. They have flowers and fruits that were an essential part of the Aboriginal diet and subsistence lifestyle. Many of these are still collected and eaten today.

Plants

Wattle *Acacia latescens*

A hardy understorey Acacia endemic to the Top End. This slender erect tree growing to between 4 and 9 m tall has narrow, pendulous leaves. The trunk has tight, finely flaky bark which may be reddish in young trees becoming dark brown to black and fissured in older trees. Most Australian Acacias (or wattles) do not have true leaves, except for a short time at the seedling stage. As the plant grows, modified stems or stalks, known as phyllodes, take the form function of leaves. The phyllodes of *Acacia latescens* are sickle-shaped and narrow (to 2 cm wide) with 2 main parallel veins. At the beginning of the dry season it produces fragrant cream flowers in globular heads composed of clusters of small fluffy balls. These may later develop into flattened woody pods containing several black seeds.

Silverleaved Wattle *Acacia holosericea*

A bushy shrub to 4 m high often found in disturbed areas, roadsides and along creek lines. This species is easily distinguished by the grey-green appearance of the foliage and branches which are covered with dense silvery hairs. The broad phyllodes are widest in the middle and slightly curved with 3 to 4 main veins, which join towards the base. In the mid dry season the yellow flowers are borne on spikes growing from the leaf axils. The distinctive papery seed pods curl up and intertwine, forming curious balls from which emerge small shiny black seeds on bright yellow arils (stalks).

Milkwood
Alstonia actinophylla

A stately, slow-growing, large tree, 15 to 20 m tall with distinctive grey corky bark and crown of small leaves. In Darwin there are many old battle-scarred Milkwoods that survived the full brunt of Cyclone Tracy to become some of the oldest street trees. The fine pointed leaves occur in whorls of 4 to 7 and contain a milky sap or latex. Although used as a medicine and as ceremonial paint by Aboriginal people, this sap can cause blindness if it comes in contact with the eyes. Masses of small white, sweetly scented flowers are formed in dense clusters on long stems during August to September and create a focus for bees and insects and a nightmare for Asthma sufferers!. Seeds are produced in paired papery pods which split open to release the numerous finely hairy seeds.

Green Plum *Buchanania obovata*

A common understorey tree in woodlands and open forest, usually untidy or straggly and between 4 and 10 m tall. The leaves are large and leathery with a rounded tip and distinct fishbone pattern of venation. The leaves show a remarkable variation in size and shape. Numerous cream flowers are produced in long terminal stalks and during October - December the tree produces small green fruits with large stones surrounded by a thin layer of sweet flesh. Ripe fruit is soft and yellow-green in colour; also known as wild mango, this fruit is good bush tucker.

Kurrajong *Brachychiton megaphyllus*

Usually an inconspicuous, deciduous tree, it is noticed when its pretty red flowers appear boldly against its bare dry season branches. Usually only 2 to 3 m tall, the Kurrajong is a common understorey plant in woodland habitats. During the dry season it drops its large dinner-plate sized leaves, exposing its dark grey trunk. Appearing much like a lifeless stump the surprising appearance of showy, bell-shaped red blooms on the branches is always intriguing. The plant produces a hard woody seed pod which splits down one side when ripe, forming a boat-like structure, and revealing pea-sized yellow, edible seeds. Both the seed pod and the seeds are covered with bristly hairs. The Kurrajong is Darwin's flower.

Cypress Pine *Callitris intratropica*

A straight-trunked tree with distinctive pine-like foliage. Bark is rough, dark grey to black and persistent to the finer branches. The leaves of the Cypress Pine are actually reduced to small scales arranged in whorls on the branchlets. Winged seeds are borne in small round cones at the ends of the branches. This species is fire-sensitive and the high incidence of fire in the Darwin region has reduced its range. Aside from scattered Cypress in woodland habitats, it is now more or less restricted to protected rocky outcrops.

Turkey Bush *Calytrix exstipulata*

During June and July, many woodland habitats are delightfully transformed by masses of showy pink-flowering Calytrix. A small, erect, evergreen shrub growing to 2 m, it is a common and widespread species in open situations. Leaves are tiny and stalkless and when crushed release the distinctive teatree-oil fragrance common to the Myrtaceae family which includes the paperbarks Melaleuca and the Eucalypts. The pink flowers are star-like. *Calytrix exstipulata* is a coloniser of rocky ground and occurs in groves on roadsides, borrow pits and disturbed ground.

Kapok Bush *Cochlospermum fraseri*

A small, slight tree to 6 m high, highly noticeable in woodland habitats during the dry season when it produces its prominent bright yellow flowers. Kapok Bush is deciduous and the plant often flowers when it has shed its large, lobed leaves. After flowering, large woody pods form which split open when ripe. The plant takes its common name from the cotton-like fibre or kapok which encloses the seeds, probably assisting with its dispersal by wind or water.

Corymbia bleeseri

A common Eucalypt in the Darwin region growing to 20 metres. Typically found on rocky rises and gravelly, shallow soils, this species is readily distinguished from other gums by its smooth whitish trunk which has persistent red and brown flakes and its shiny leaves. Flowering occurs during April-June and the showy bunches of white flowers are a rich source of nectar for native bees. The fruits are on long stalks and form rounded, urn-shaped woody capsules.

Cycad *Cycas armstrongii*

Cycads are an ancient group that, although palm-like in appearance, are actually very closely related to the pines or conifers. The slender, dark-grey trunk is actually made up of closely packed leaf bases. This is topped by a dense arrangement of stiff, sharp-pointed fronds.

Cycads are highly noticeable after dry season fires, when, in contrast to the blackened landscape, they throw out a full head of soft, furry leaves which are a stunning bright green. Male plants produce a large oval cone, composed of numerous scales, at the apex of the trunk. Female plants produce egg-shaped, hard woody seeds on pendulous spikes. *Cycas armstrongii* is a species characteristic of woodlands in the Darwin region and is well adapted to the harsh environment. This species is deciduous and survives the Dry in a dormant leafless form. A surprisingly large underground tuber is the energy source which enables it to produce a whole new canopy of leaves within a few days of fire.

67

Darwin Woollybutt *Eucalyptus miniata*

One of the most common tree species in the Darwin region and right across the Top End. The Woollybutt as the name implies has thick, dark, flaky bark on the lower trunk, with the upper branches left smooth and white. Woollybutts usually grow to 20 m or less in height and tend to occur on relatively shallow or gravelly yellow soils. Large orange-red flowers are produced amongst the new season's foliage during May to July. Fruit capsules are stout, ribbed woody gumnuts that may have a white waxy covering particularly in the drier parts of its range.

Ghost Gum *Corymbia bella*

Ghost gums as a group which includes this species, range from New Guinea to central Australia. A moderate-sized tree to 15 m, it has a shapely smooth white trunk, occasionally with a short scarf of flaky grey bark towards the base of the tree. Leaves of the Darwin variety are long and thin

with wavy margins. Small white flowers and thin-walled papery fruits form on long pedicels or stalks during the dry season. In the Darwin area, ghost gums can be found on the sandy levees of streams and fringing billabongs and grassy coastal plains.

Darwin Stringybark *Eucalyptus tetrodonta*

Darwin Stringybark is found from the Kimberley to Cape York and is a dominant tree species of open forest in the Darwin area. An erect tall tree to 30 m, the trunk and branches have grey fibrous bark throughout. Leaves are lanceolate (curved sides tapering to a pointed tip). White flowers in groups of three form in the leaf axils in the mid dry season, developing into bell-shaped woody nuts up to 2 cm long. The flower buds and gum nuts have 4 small teeth around the upper rim which gives this tree its name (tetra, four; donta, teeth). The tree develops its best form on deeper red soils where it occurs in pure stands. Usually, however, it grows in association with Darwin Woollybutt.

Ironwood *Erythrophleum chlorostachys*

A common tree 12 to 15 m tall, widespread in many well-drained habitats and endemic to tropical Australia. The corky bark of young trees becomes dark grey and coarsely tessellated in larger trees. Ironwood has compound leaves composed of small leaflets (2 to 4 cm) which are rounded and leathery. In dry locations the tree is partly deciduous. When new foliage is produced, just before the wet season, it is a vibrant pale green, later developing into a dark green spreading crown. Creamy coloured flowers on short spikes appear amongst the new growth during August to November. Large flattened woody pods, containing 4 to 8 very hard seeds, are retained on the trees for many months after ripening. Ironwood is well known for its extremely hard and durable, dark red timber which is also termite resistant. Aboriginal people have multiple uses for this species including carving the wood for spear heads, digging and ceremonial sticks. Infusions of the bark are used for pain relief and preparations from the roots are used as an antiseptic for cuts and sores. Its foliage is poisonous to stock and all parts of the tree are poisonous to mammals.

Bushman's Peg *Grevillea decurrens*

A common Grevillea in open forest and woodland particularly in undulating, stony country, endemic to the Northern Territory. A slender tree 3 to 5 m high with leaves divided into 2 to 5 pairs of pinnate-like lobes. Each leaf lobe has a distinctive mid-vein and a rounded tip. Flowering occurs during the wet season when pale pink spikes are produced in loose clusters. Rounded, woody nuts split open to release a pair of papery seeds. This species may be confused with *Grevillea heliosperma*, also a slender tree within Eucalyptus forest. *G. heliosperma* is typically a taller plant with narrower leaf lobes, and less distinct veins, and with reddish, rather than pinkish, flowers which appear during the dry season.

Fern-leaved Grevillea *Grevillea pteridifolia*

A widespread and common Grevillea in woodlands, particularly on sandy soils and along drainage lines. A slight tree to 8 m tall, it has distinctive silvery foliage and showy orange flowers. The leaves are finely divided, dark green above, and covered with silky silver hairs beneath - this bilateral difference in colouring is very noticeable on a windy dry season day. Profuse displays of orange blossoms during the early to mid-dry season attract many nectivorous birds, insects and mammals. Aboriginal people traditionally used the copious nectar shaken from the flowers to sweeten drinking water. Small, furry, oval shaped nuts are later formed, containing paired seeds. *Grevillea pteridifolia* can tolerate periods of flooding and is often found growing in pure stands on the fringes of floodplains and along the banks of permanent freshwater streams.

Sand Palm *Livistona humilis*

A common and widespread fan palm typically found within the understorey layer of eucalypt forest where it may form dense stands. Growing to a maximum of 5 m, it has a hairy to rough grey trunk, ringed with old leaf bases. The leaves are stiff and fan shaped with numerous pointed lobes. Yellow flowers are held on long arching spikes during September to May. These stalks also support the purple-black seeds. Aboriginal people extract a purple or black dye from the fruit and shoots. The central growing shoot of the palm can also be eaten raw or roasted. A similar species of small fan-palm, *Livistona inermis*, can be distinguished from *L. humilis* by its deeply divided leaf lobes (more than three-quarters length) which are usually drooping. *Livistona inermis* characteristically grows in sandstone country and rocky escarpments and not on the plains.

Owenia vernicosa

A small tree 4 to 12 m tall, with an open crown, usually occurring as an understorey tree in open forest and woodland. The slender trunks have dark rough bark. The tree has distinctive compound leaves measuring over 30 cm long comprised of 15 to 30 leaflets. The leaves are bunched towards the end of the branches and the tree is semi-deciduous. Owenia has male and female trees. Female flowers develop reddish pendulous fruits on long stalks. The apple-like fruits have thin flesh enclosing a hard stony seed. Old pitted seeds are often found clustered around the base of the tree. Aboriginal people use the bark and leaves of this species as a fish poison and preparations made from bark shavings were used to treat coughs.

Milky Plum Tree *Persoonia falcata*

A small tree 3 to 5 m tall, with rough, grey, flaky bark. It is a common shrub or tree, often mistaken for an Acacia. Leaves alternate, smooth, leathery and dull with wavy margins. New fine hairy tips alert you with their bright reddish colour. Yellow, tubular flowers are produced June through September. The fruits are edible when they have yellowed usually from November to February.

Quinine Tree *Petalostigma pubescens*

A small evergreen tree to 6 m tall with rough finely fissured grey bark. It is a common mid-stratum species with small ovate leaves, shiny green above and finely hairy beneath. Male and female flowers are borne on separate trees, and are cream-coloured and inconspicuous. Large bright orange globular fruits (to 2 cm in diameter) break open explosively into several segments when ripe. Timber from Quinine Tree makes good firewood and Aboriginal people fashioned the wood to make spear-throwers. The species has traditional medicinal value - a preparation made from the fruits was used by women to prevent conception, and whole fruits were placed in the mouth to relieve toothache. The common name appears to relate to the plant's bitter taste rather than its chemical properties.

Cocky Apple *Planchonia careya*

A shrubby small tree to 8 m, common on a variety of soil types. The leaves are smooth, pale green and ovate with slightly serrated edges. The leaves are shiny above with a dull, paler undersurface. Planchonia is semi-deciduous and the leaves often turn a bright red before falling. Large showy pink and white flowers comprise little more than a circlet of numerous waxy stamens to 6 cm in length. The flowers are short-lived and may open at night since the flowers are often seen on the ground by mid-morning. Many species with similar night-opening, stamenous flowers are pollinated by nocturnal animals such as bats and moths.

Red Bush Apple *Syzygium suborbiculare*

A common medium-sized tree to 12 m high with distinctive large, round, glossy leaves (suborbiculare refers to the almost orbicular leaf shape). Red Bush Apple grows as an evergreen understorey tree with rough, dark-grey bark in eucalypt-dominated open forest and produces showy white flowers, composed of numerous stamens, during July to October. Around November, large globular, red fruits appear, similar in appearance to a small ribbed apple. Like a number of Asian species of Syzygium, the fruits are edible but usually tart in flavour. Medicinal properties are reported for the leaves, bark, fruit and seed of this species.

Billy goat Plum, Kakadu Plum *Terminalia ferdinandiana*

A small to medium-sized tree with large, rounded, almost circular leaves. Reaching 4 to 10 m in height, this species is a very common understorey species, deciduous during the dry season. The leaves are characteristically crowded toward the ends of the branches and arranged spirally on the stems. Tiny white flowers on spikes to 20 cm long appear amongst the new foliage at the beginning of the wet season. Characteristically, the fruits are fleshy green-yellow drupes with a small beak. They are good bush tucker, available for eating from March onwards. Research has shown that they have an exceptionally high Vitamin C content.

Xanthostemon paradoxus

A small, often crooked, evergreen tree, 4 to 12 m high, found scattered in a variety of habitats from moist sites to rocky ridges and throughout Eucalyptus dominated woodlands. It has rough, grey bark that peels in flakes, and has hard dense timber, used by Aboriginal people for digging sticks. Leaves are variable in shape but generally oval, being widest in the centre. Leaves are crowded toward the ends of the branches and young leaves may be grey-green and finely hairy becoming a dark shiny green. Dense clusters of bright yellow flowers with numerous stamens are produced at the ends of the branches sporadically throughout the year. Rounded woody capsules break open into 3 to 4 segments when brown and ripe. Xanthostemon is a member of the Myrtaceae family which includes Eucalyptus and Melaleuca, and one of three Xanthostemon species in the Darwin Region.

One of the most conspicuous stick-insects found in the Top End is a species of Eurycnema. This impressive insect has a body length of around 25 cm. It is green with a flush of red under the forewings which it flashes when disturbed, arching its abdomen upward to enhance the effect. The insect is not dangerous and prefers to be left alone to feed quietly on acacias.

ANIMALS OF THE WOODLANDS AND OPEN FOREST

Birds

The Top End is rich in birds, with over 250 different species recorded for the region. Forty four of these birds, or 17%, occupy open forests and woodlands as a primary habitat, but more than half of the total avifauna use the open forests and woodlands. Because woodlands are widespread outside the Top End, so are many of the birds. Examples of widespread birds are the Red-tailed Black Cockatoos and the White-winged Trillers. Species that are confined to northern Australia include the Partridge Pigeons and Long-tailed Finches, which thrive on the rich understorey grasses that are a feature of the northern woodlands. It is however the supply of nectar and insects that largely controls the number and types of birds. In the woodlands and forests, nearly two-thirds of all birds forage for these resources.

Most of the 18 species of honeyeaters in the Top End are to some extent nectarivorous, and consequently respond to the flowering of nectar-producing trees in different habitats. The Brown Honeyeater moves between open forest and riparian habitats in search of nectar, whereas the Banded Honeyeater and the Rufous-throated Honeyeater remain in the open forests and woodlands. Whenever trees or shrubs are flowering, as many as six species of nectarivorous can be seen squabbling over the flowers. These include the Brown Honeyeater, the White-throated Honeyeater, the Banded Honeyeater and the Little Friarbird. The more common birds or characteristically Top End birds of the open forests and woodland are described below.

Birds of the woodlands

Black Kite *Milvus migrans*

The most common raptor in the Darwin area, the Black Kite is about 52 cm long, with a wingspan of 1.2 m. It has a forked tail, which it constantly twists and turns to stabilise itself. The plumage is a dark, muddy brown with fine, dark streaks. The Black Kite is frequently confused with the larger Whistling Kite, which is paler, does not twist its tail as much, and does not flock in such large numbers. The Black Kite is typically flying and soars effortlessly on wings that are held flat. It is an extremely gregarious bird, seldom seen alone. They have strong scavenging tendencies and flocks of hundreds are not uncommon and they quickly appear in number as soon as bushfires start. The call is a plaintive descending 'see-err" and whistling si-i-i-i".

Whistling Kite *Haliastur sphenurus*

This is a common and widespread kite, which soars effortlessly. Its plumage is light brown with plentiful pale streaks on its head, back and breast. It has pale spots on its upper parts. The bird can be mistaken for the Black Kite, which is about the same length, but in flight the underwing pattern is distinctive with the pale forepart of the wing joining a cream band that crosses the wing near the tip, leaving a large, dark rectangle along the trailing edge. The Whistling Kites does not flock in such great numbers as does the Black, nor manoeuvre its tail as much. It has a distinctive shrill, whistling call; the first note leisurely, long and descending followed, by a quick upward burst of four to six short, shrill staccato notes. The Whistling Kite feeds mainly on carrion and can be seen in large numbers around bushfires.

Brown Falcon *Falco berigora*

This 50 cm long bird has a wingspan of less than a metre. It is one of the most widespread and abundant raptors. Its plumage is variable and it can be mistaken for a number of other raptors. Two features, however, are constant: a double moustache mark enclosing a paler cheek-patch; and buff to pale red-brown notching of flight and tail feathers. In flight its wings are held up in a V-shape. The Brown Falcon's main method of searching for food is to sit quietly on a high perch, dropping down on victims. Usually seen alone or in pairs, it is the noisiest of Australian raptors with screeches and a demented, hoarse cackling.

Nankeen Kestrel *Falco cenchroides*

The Nankeen Kestrel is a small falcon, about 30 cm long, with a wingspan of 75 cm. It hunts in a distinctive manner, hovering - almost hanging - in mid-air at one spot for minutes at a time, watching the ground with wings quivering and tail fanned. When it sees prey it drops in steps and then plummets head first onto the victim. It has pale rufous upper parts with contrasting black flight feathers and whitish underparts. The voice is shrill rapid-fire 'kikikikikiki'.

Partridge Pigeon *Geophaps smithii*

A striking, ground feeding, bronze-winged pigeon with obvious red skin around the eye, growing to about 26 cm long. Flocks of up to 20 or so birds explode into flight when disturbed. It keeps to open woodland, well-grassed with sorghum (speargrass) where they feed. It is sometimes seen hurrying across roads particularly when the grass is tall. It walks from place to place keeping contact with soft coos. Numbers of this bird are decreasing.

Peaceful Dove *Geopelia placida*

A common grey-brown dove with barred mantle and neck. At 20 cm it is the smaller of the two most common doves in Darwin. Feeds on seeds on the ground in pairs and small parties, flushes with a 'frrr' of the wings, never flying far. Its voice is a characteristic 'doodle-doo', repeated monotonously.

Bar-shouldered Dove *Geopelia humeralis*

A large brown dove, with barred, copper-coloured nape and barred wings. At 29 cm it is the larger of the two most common doves in Darwin. Usually seen in small groups, but larger groups may occur at the end of the dry season, congregating around food which can be bulbs of sedges or seeds. Always feed on the ground, and often associated with pandanus. Voice high pitched melodious 'coolicoo', emphatic 'hook, coo! hook, coo!' and jumbled, laughing coos.

Galah *Cacatua roseicapilla*

The Galah is one of Australia's most loved and most beautiful birds. A medium-sized pink and grey cockatoo, about 36 cm, it is pale grey above, rose-pink to deep rose-red below, with low cap-like crest. This bird is usually seen in flocks of 30 to 1000. The flight of the Galah, much loved by cartoonists, is a continuous, deep flapping, swaying from side to side (like a silly Galah!). It is a seed-eater and its call is a single-note contact screech, to harsh screeching at other times.

Red-tailed Black Cockatoo *Calyptorhynchus banksii*

The only black cockatoo in the Darwin region, large up to 66 cm. The male is black all over except for the broad, scarlet panels in the tail, which are conspicuous when taking off and landing. The female is black with yellow spots and yellow bars on her underparts. Her tail panels are yellow-orange. The Red-tailed Black Cockatoo flies with funereal wing-beats, almost rowing through the sky. They are found

in pairs, family groups or small parties, feeding high in the trees on seeds and can also be seen in burnt areas eating seeds from the ground. Semi-nomadic, they appear in the Darwin area and Top End in the early dry season. Trumpet-like calls of 'cree-cree' carry far and sound slightly mournful, reminiscent of a rusty hinge and also a deep 'growk'.

Sulphur-crested Cockatoo *Cacatua leadbeateri*

This white, well-known cockatoo is about 50 cm and sports a sulphur-yellow crest. The underwing and undertail is washed yellow. In northern Australia small parties are the usual social unit. It occurs in a variety of wooded habitats, rarely far from trees. Each day the birds fly at a considerable height, to a feeding site, and feed on the ground on seeds, bulbs and grasses, until around mid-morning when they adjourn to nearby trees to strip the leaves and bark, looking for insects and their larvae. In the afternoon they return to their roosting tree to screech raucously in a shattering manner to each other. This is a common sound in and around Darwin.

Red-collared Lorikeet *Trichoglossus rubritorquis*

This is the common, fast flying parrot of the Darwin region. Large dark-green lorikeet, about 30 cm, with a blue head, orange breast and collar. Often seen at dawn or dusk flying in small parties, moving like arrows, on pointed whirring wings, screeching regularly. The birds are acrobatic feeders, using their brush-like tongues to mop up nectar on any nectar-bearing plant from eucalypts to cultivated trees. They also eat insects and fruit on occasion and roost noisily in flocks. The birds screech and chatter continuously.

Red-winged Parrot *Aprosmictus erythropterus*

A bright green parrot, about 32 cm, with a red bill and red on the wing. The back is black and there is a concealed blue patch on the rump. In pairs or in small family groups, it usually comes to ground only to drink. Sometimes seen flying over Darwin, the flight is erratic with swooping undulations. It feed on seeds, blossoms, fruits and buds. The voice is a metallic 'ching, ching, ching'.

Pheasant Coucal *Centropus phasianinus*

The coucal is not a pheasant. This large, up to 66 cm, rather ungainly bird with a long tail, often carried erect or spread, is actually a cuckoo, known to Aboriginal people all over the Top End as Bukbuk (book book). The coucal is unusual in being the only Australian non-parasitic cuckoo, constructing a domed nest made of grass and rearing up to five young. It is a dark bird with streaks, more often heard than seen, as it skulks in dense undergrowth. It characteristically dashes across roads and clearings and when flushed, flies reluctantly and takes comical poses as it crash-lands untidily or flops into cover. Its diet includes frogs, lizards and insects, which it hunts within grassland, and occasionally takes eggs and nestlings. The booming, whooping call of the coucal is a sure indicator of the change of season, often uncannily linked with the first rains. Its deep, hollow 'coo-coo-coo-coo-coo-coo-coocal' begins slowly and accelerates.

Torresian Crow *Corvus orru*

The only crow that occurs across northern Australia. Glossy black, and about 50 cm, it shuffles its wings exaggeratedly when alighting. A rather shy crow, it prefers areas with tall trees. Torresian Crows eat carrion, insects and plant material. Can be seen in flocks of 50 or so, but established pairs hold a permanent territory. Voice is an 'uk-uk-uk-uk-uk' or 'ok-ok-ok' or 'oh-oh-oh-oh' - never an 'a' like the Australian Raven.

Blue-winged Kookaburra *Dacelo leachii*

The tropical relative of the well-known southern Laughing Kookaburra, this slightly smaller kookaburra, 38-42 cm, does not laugh, but produces raucous, frantic howls. A large, heavy kingfisher, twice the size of any other kingfisher in the Darwin region, with a characteristic heavy bill and mainly blue wings. Kookaburras nest in tree hollows (paperbarks and woollybutts are especially favoured) and live in extended, territorial, family groups of 2 to 10 birds. Often using exposed perches such as dead trees and power lines, it sits motionless with tail cocked and bill pointing downward, waiting for their prey, which the bird dives onto. It has an unmistakable voice, which starts off with a guttural 'klock, klock, klock' and develops into a cacophony of squarks and screeches that gets louder and louder, often ending in a series of chuckles usually made by several birds in unison.

Sacred Kingfisher *Halcyon sancta*

A small kingfisher, about 19 to 23 cm., the male has blue shoulders, a bright blue rump and bright, deep blue tail with collar and underparts white. The female is larger, duller and greener. The Sacred Kingfisher is a land-living kingfisher and is usually solitary. Its diet is mainly small reptiles, crickets, grasshoppers, beetles and their larvae. It spends much of its time sitting very quietly on a low branch looking down for prey which they plunge onto. The voice is a distinctive descending 'kik-kik-kik-kik-kik'.

Rainbow Bee-eater *Merops ornatus*

Australia's only bee-eater, this is a gorgeous, pale green and blue bird, about 23 cm. It has a fine-curved black bill, blue-edged, black eye-mark and a pale orange throat with

a black mark in the centre. The males' two central tail feathers extend like wires to 25 to 50 mm. The female has shorter tail feathers. These birds are communal, travelling in groups of 20 or 30. They are also migratory, leaving Darwin during the wet season and returning in March or April. Migrating as far north as Papua New Guinea and into Indonesia. Rainbow Bee-eaters catch food on the wing, sallying forth from branches. They eat flying insects including wasps and bees. They are elegant, acrobatic fliers with broad but pointed wings. Their voice is a melodious 'trrrp, trrrp', usually heard when on the wing.

Dollarbird *Eurystomus orientalis*

This red-billed stocky bird, 30 cm, has pale blue wing spots in flight (the 'dollar'). Upperparts are brown, with a blue throat and wings green-blue, and it has a characteristic silhouette of broad head, short neck and stumpy tail. A tropical bird which spends the dry season in Papua New Guinea and adjacent islands, it migrates to Australia for the wet season. A solitary bird, or in pairs, mostly noticed perching prominently on tall, dead trees or telephone wires. From there it sallies out for flying insects. Voice is a loud rasping 'yap, yapapapapa' usually directed to the mate.

Black-faced Cuckoo-shrike *Coracina novaehollandiae*

Neither cuckoo nor shrike, the cuckoo-shrikes take their name from their cuckoo-like form and shrike-like bill. The Black-faced Cuckoo-shrike is about 33 cm and is a widespread and familiar bird, mainly visiting during the dry season in Darwin. It is smokey-grey with a distinctive black face and throat, grading rapidly into white below. It is found in pairs to family groups, foraging on insects, fruits and even nesting birds. Their flight is of long, graceful undulations and when they land they have the characteristic habit of repeatedly refolding their wings, hence their other common name 'shuffle-wing'. The voice is a plaintive 'plee-urk' or pleasant chirring.

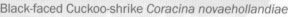

White-winged Triller *Lalage sueurii*

These are migratory birds, up to 18 cm. The male and female have different plumage. The breeding male is glossy black above with a grey rump and pure white below. It has conspicuous white shoulders and white edges to the wing feathers. Non-breeding males black back and crown are replaced with brown. The female is brown above and off-white below with buff wing and head markings. The White-winged Triller moves south of the Tropic of Capricorn during the wet season, returning in March-April. Trillers usually travel as groups of 3 to 50. The group forages on beetles, grasshoppers, phasmids and other insects. Flight is swift and graceful with long, looping undulations. The song, uttered by the male during breeding season, is a loud, incessant, musical chatter 'chif-chif-chif-joey-joey-joey' ending in a canary-like trill.

Rufous Whistler *Pachycephala rufiventris*

There Is scarcely a tract of open forest anywhere without a Rufous Whistler. About 17 cm, the male is grey above with a blackish mask extending down the side of the neck and joining like a broad necklace separating the white throat from the rufous underparts. The female is brownish-grey above and pale buff below with dark streaks. Occurring mostly alone or in pairs, the birds hop methodically from branch to branch taking insects and larvae and occasionally berries. The voice is a loud, vigorous 'ee-chong, joey-joey' often heard after a loud noise, like slamming a car door; it also calls a plaintive 'sweet'.

Willie Wagtail *Rhipidura leucophrys*

A black and white fantail, about 20 cm. One of Australia's favourite birds, it has a glossy black head, upper chest, upperparts and long tail. Underparts and prominent eyebrows, white. Tail is cocked jauntily and twitched from side to side, and fanned out to flush out insects. Hunts in ones or twos on the ground in a series of hops or zigzagging flights. Prefers open spaces and is common throughout Australia, except for dense forest. Voice is a 'sweet pretty creature' song or a scolding 'chick-a-chick-a-chick'. Often heard on moonlit nights.

Golden-headed Cisticola *Cisticola exilis*

A little, 10 cm, golden-brown, grass bird. Tail is longer in the dry season. The head of the male in the wet season becomes golden, losing its black streaks. Usually an inconspicuous bird, which feeds on insects on the ground beneath grass swards in groups. But in the breeding season, at the beginning of the wet season, the males rise to fly out from exposed places to jerk and undulate at around 10-20 metres high, before pitching to cover. The male utters incessant, far-carrying, insect-like calls 'bhzzt' followed by a loud 'pleek' during the mating season.

Silver-crowned Friarbird *Philemon argenticeps*

This large, 30 cm, honeyeater has a prominent, gently sloping knob at the forehead. Crown, forehead and nape silvery white. The bare facial skin is dark grey, upperparts pale brown and underparts a pale colour. A common bird in and around Darwin, avoiding the denser forests, it feeds noisily in upper foliage of eucalypts and paperbarks, for nectar, insects and fruit. The bird is locally nomadic, following flushes of flowering, noisily clanking and chuckling when they establish their small feeding territories. Nest is often parasitised by the Koel. One of the first voices of the dawn chorus is the unmistakable rolling clanking, 'more tobacco, uh-more tobacco-uh', often in duet.

Blue-faced Honeyeater *Entomyzon cyanotis*

A large, 30 cm, honeyeater with a striking blue-coloured patch of facial skin around the eye. Golden green upper parts and white underparts. It is a bird of the open and mixed forest. Common in Darwin, the birds work communally, rifling nectar from flowers, taking insects and sometimes fruit. This is a bold bird, coming down to feed in gardens or rubbish tips and given to noisy displays. Its voice is strident and distinct. A common call is a penetrating 'woik, woik' or 'queet, queet'.

Little Friarbird *Philemon citreogularis*

Smaller than the Silver-crowned Friarbird, about 25 cm, and with no knob, this bird has bare, slate-grey facial skin, a grey-brown head and upperparts and pale underparts. Common in the open forests away from Darwin the bird focuses on smaller flowering areas, rarely visited by the larger friarbirds. It is a local nomad, following the flowers. Its voice is more musical than other birds, though also raucous 'ar-cooo, rockety crook-shank'.

Yellow-throated Miner *Manorina flavigula*

The Yellow-throated Miner is a 25 to 28 cm bird, with rump and whole undersurface whitish. The crown is grey and a black mark extends from the bill to under the eye and over the ear. The forehead and neck are washed yellow and there is an obvious patch of yellow skin behind the eye. Seen in groups of a dozen or so, it has strong legs and sharp claws and use these to hang in bizarre postures. It also hops about in the trees and bushes taking seeds and nectar, and on the ground looking for insects. It has a complex vocabulary of twitterings and squeaks but the commonest call is a querulous 'teee....teeee....teee'.

White-throated Honeyeater *Melithreptus brevirostris*

A small, 15 cm, green and white honeyeater with a black head. A widespread bird of the more open woodlands, in Darwin it may be seen in small groups in older eucalypts, gleaning insects and nectar in the high outer foliage. Its voice is 'tserp, tserp'; 'pi-pi-pi'.

Brown Honeyeater *Lichmera indistincta*

The Brown Honeyeater is a 15 to 19 cm, plain, olive-brown honeyeater, with a longish, curved bill and a tiny yellowish and silvery-white spot behind the eye. This small, indistinct honeyeater has a rich and varied musical song. Brown honeyeaters are opportunistic nectar-feeders. When there is no flowering the birds turn to insects, catching them among the foliage or in mid-air bursts from the high branches.

JB

Crimson Finch *Neochmia phaeton*

The male has a grey crown and nape. He has a long tapered tail. The female has a brownish-olive head and wings. She has a crimson face, beak and tail. They establish large individual territories. Males show possible nest sites to females but she ultimately decides and they have a ceremony to confirm the place. Watch out for these chattering birds in Pandanus trees.

Mistletoe-bird *Dicaeum hirundinaceum*

A tiny bird, 10 cm, the male is brightly coloured, glossy blue-black above, with the chest, throat and under the base of the tail a bright scarlet. The female is grey above with whitish underparts. The base of her tail is pale, washed red. The Mistletoe-bird has a specialised diet of the sticky mistletoe fruit, though it will take other fruit and insects occasionally. Mistletoe-birds forage along mistletoe, flying from one clump to the next in a high bullet-like flight. The call is a high-pitched, sharp, whistled 'szit' or 'dzee' in contact with other birds. It also has a distinctive song, which involves two or three rising and falling whistling notes, 'wait-a-bit, wait-a-bit'. The bird is also a mimic.

Striated Pardalote *Pardalotus striatus*

A pretty little, 10 cm, rather stumpy looking bird with a black head, and a red spot at the base of the bill, yellow throat and olive back. The wings are black with white edging. There is a bright red spot on the wing coverts. Underparts are white. It is mainly a dry season visitor to Darwin, favouring open woodlands and open gardens. As well as nesting in trees, the birds excavate nests in creek banks, road-cuttings, even excavation sites, the nest a chamber at the end of a tunnel about 60 cm long. Can be found in loose flocks of up to 100 birds. The birds fly, high and bullet-like, from tree to tree. They forage for insects, running along the branches like mice. The voice is loud and repetitive, 'pick, pick', 'pick-it-up', 'wittachew'.

Double-barred Finch *Taeniopygia guttata*

A brown-backed finch with two black bars on its breast, about 11 cm. Its face is white and its black wings are spotted white. This is the common finch found in the Darwin area. Never far from water, flocks of around 40 birds are found in scrub, edges of woodland, overgrown blocks, parks and gardens. The birds feed energetically on the ground, picking up fallen seeds and hopping up to pluck grain from seedheads. Insects are also taken. Groups flit to the nearest thicket for cover. Voice is a nasal squeak.

Long-tailed Finch *Poephila acuticauda*

A red-billed finch with a grey head, black bib, white rump and a long tail, about 15 cm. Restricted to tropical northern Australia where it is quite common in woodlands, especially along creek lines. Highly social, it lives in flocks of around 30 birds, feeding on the ground on seeds. It pair-bonds strongly, with pairs never far from one another, and seen preening each other after landing in a tree. Voice is a soft 'tet' and loud, pure whistle and soft flute-like whistles.

Olive-backed *Oriole sagittatus*

A greenish bird, about 28 cm, with a slender, slightly curved, pink bill and black-streaked, white underparts. The male is greener than the female. A woodland species, which visits Darwin gardens in the dry season, the birds feed in the upper foliage, often on fruit, but insects will also be taken. The voice is a distinctive rolling, mellow 'olly, olly, olio, orry-ole'. It is also a mimic.

Pee-Wee *Grallina cyanoleuca*

A black and white bird, 27 cm, with insistent calls, this is one of the best known and most widespread birds in Australia. Male has white eyebrow and black throat. Female has white face and throat. More common in the Darwin region in the dry season, it is found in pairs. A bird of the open spaces, it feeds mainly on the ground, often at the edge of water, on insects and larvae. When walking, the head bobs back and forth in time with the feet. The birds build a mud nest in tree hollows, and tree branches. The voice is the well known 'pee-wee', which reflects the other common name for the bird, Peewee.

White-breasted Woodswallow *Artamus leucorhynchus*

A stoutly build bird, 17 cm, with long wings and blue bill tipped black. Dark grey with white breast and rump, it is the only woodswallow without a white tip to the tail. Woodswallows are soaring birds, which feed on insects and are common around Darwin in the dry season. Occurring in groups of up to a hundred, the birds have the endearing habit of cuddling up to one another when roosting. The voice is a brisk 'pirt, pirt'. Also a soft pleasant song, and it is a mimic.

Pied Butcherbird *Cracticus nigrogularis*

A conspicuous, 35 cm, black and white bird, with a pure and glorious voice. The white body is set off by a wholly black head, throat and upper breast. The wings and back are black, except for a conspicuous white panel on the wings. The straight bill is finely hooked at the tip. It hunts by perch-and-pounce, in a wide habitat range, picking off insects, reptiles, small mammals and even other birds. It flys swiftly from point-to-point and swoop up to a new perch. Its voice is a slow flute-like piping.

Grey Butcherbird *Cracticus torquatus*

A smaller butcherbird, up to 30 cm, than the Pied, white-throated with grey back and greyish wash on upperparts. Like the Pied Butcherbird, it lives in open woodland but preferring taller woodlands than the Pied. It is less obvious than the Pied. In other respects it is like the Pied Butcherbird. Voice also a beautiful deep, mellow piping.

Tawny Frogmouth *Podargus strigoides*

The most common nocturnal bird in the Darwin region and widespread around Australia, is not at all related to owls. Often seen in the car headlights this 34-46 cm bird has large yellow eyes, otherwise tawny-grey coloured, marbled and streaked. Known as a 'frogmouth' because of its wide bill, the bird swoops from low branches or along roadsides for large nocturnal insects and spiders. This behaviour means that it is often a road casualty. In the day it disguises itself as part of a dead branch by sitting completely still with its bill pointed skyward and its eyes slitted almost completely closed. Its call 'ooom-oom-oom-oom-oom', can be heard when it is the mating season, as the rains approach and the termites are released from their nests.

Barking Owl *Ninox connivens*

Large, bright yellow eyes. Upperparts brownish-grey, coarsely spotted white. Flight feathers, tail barred lighter. Underparts white, streaked brownish-grey.
Male larger. Call is like a barking dog. Lives around forests and woodlands.

Australian Owlet-nightjar *Aegotheles cristatus*

Bill black. Black collar. Pink feet. Underparts, tail grey, finely barred and blackish. Large brown eye that is non-reflective to lights. Head has wide black eye-stripes that meet behind and extend to crown. Found in woodlands with tree hollows.

Spotted Nightjar *Eurostopodus argus*

White throat. Large white wing spot. Rounded wings. Bill black. Eye brown.
Pointed wings. Dark grey above with black, sandy and whitish spots, patches, bars. Lives around open forests, woodlands and monsoon vine thickets.

Barn Owl *Tyto alba*

Small black eyes. Rounded heart-shaped mask with brown border. Underparts white, sparsely dark-flecked. Long unfeathered lower legs protrude in flight. Lives in grasslands, woodlands, farms. May roost on ground or in caves.

Frill-necked Lizard in defensive display *Chlamydosaurus kingii*

Reptiles

More than 80 species of lizards, snakes, turtles, and frogs can be found in the forests and woodlands of the Darwin region. Perhaps the most flamboyant of the reptiles is the Frill-necked Lizard. Others such as the Black-headed Python and the Gould's Goanna are very distinctive, while others still are cryptic and live on and under leaf litter or burrow under the sand and soil. Walkers in the forests and woodlands will notice the rustling activity of lizards, such as the rainbow skink, *Carlia*, amongst the leaf litter. Unfortunately goannas, especially *Varanus panoptes*, King Brown snakes, Death Adder snakes are not so commonly seen since cane toads have hopped in to invade Darwin and the Top End of the NT.

Measuring reptiles – finding the vent

Many skinks and geckoes easily lose their tails when handled or frightened. Most dragons and goannas and all snakes keep theirs. Because herpetologists needed a standard to measure lizard and snakes lengths, they chose measures that would always be present, much as birds and mammals are measured by their head-body length. For lizards and snakes, this became the snout-vent length or SVL. The vent is the scale covering the anal opening just forward of the tail. The vent can be located by turning the snake or lizard over, and looking just to the rear of the legs in skinks, and towards the end of the body in snakes. Snakes have very short tails in comparison with body length, whereas many lizards have natural tails as long as, and some much longer than, their snout-vent lengths. The vent can be single or divided, and is usually slightly different from the other scales of the body and tail.

The descriptions in this book use the snout-vent length or SVL, as this is the standard, except for goannas (varanids), and larger snakes where the total length is given.

Black-headed Python *Aspidites melanocephalus*

Skinks

Many of the skinks, which inhabit the Darwin area are small and fast, rustling the leaves, or causing a flash of movement or colour. Some groups are commonly found in similar habitats, such as always in the leaf litter, or always on trees or rocks. To help keen observers of these small, but significant, animals, we have arranged them in rough groupings. Proper identification can be made by using Paul Horner's excellent book Skinks of the Northern Territory, or the herpetologist's bible Reptiles and Amphibians of Australia by Harold Cogger.

Douglas' Skink
Glaphyromorphus douglasi

The two *Glaphyromorphus* skinks are very shiny, looking as if they have been freshly lacquered. They are larger than the common Carlias and Menetias and have substantial tails which are longer than their bodies.

Douglas' Skink is a medium-sized (80 millimetre SVL) robust skink inhabiting Darwin woodlands, forests, coasts and gardens. They are medium to dark brown, occasionally with spots on the body. Douglas' Skinks are usually found in moist areas, but sometimes under cover on beaches. They range from western Arnhem Land to Van Diemen Gulf and on Melville Island. They are often seen wrestling for territory, and are most active in the cool of the day.

Darwin Skink *Glaphyromorphus darwiniensis*

This common but secretive skink is up to 58 millimetres from snout to vent, with a solid tail longer than its head-body or snout-vent length. The Darwin Skink has very short limbs, and is usually coloured light to rich brown. They mostly live in thick leaf litter in natural closed forest and woodland and in gardens. It is found from Arnhem Land to the Kimberley.

Northern Blue-tongued Lizard
Tiliqua scincoides intermedia

The Blue-tongue is a large, heavy skink 370 millimetres long. It is usually rich brown above, with obscure pale transverse stripes. Found across the northern Kimberley and the Top End, it occupies open forest and woodland, and feeds on insects, spiders, snails and also plant material such as flowers, fruits and berries.

Little Skinks

Differences between *Carlia* and *Menetia*, and *Morethia* and *Cryptoblepharus*, and *Notoscincus* and *Proablepharus*. These genera of skinks look very similar in the field. The first difference to notice is the number of fingers (on the front foot). *Carlia* and *Menetia* have 4 fingers, while *Morethia*, *Cryptoblepharus*, *Notoscincus* and *Proablepharus* have 5 fingers.

The next difference between *Carlia* and *Menetia* is the eyelid. In Menetias the lower eyelid is fused to the upper, making a permanent transparent spectacle. Carlias have a movable lower eyelid, like ours, which moves over the eye. The lower eyelid has a large transparent disk. The other four Genera have fused eyelids, which is why they are commonly called snake-eyed skinks. *Cryptoblepharus* lives on trees and rocks, running rapidly over the surface. *Morethia* and the other 4 skinks live on the ground and amongst leaf litter.

Rainbow skinks

Two-spined Rainbow Skink	*Carlia amax*	to 40mm
Slender Rainbow Skink	*Carlia gracilis*	to 40mm
Red-sided Rainbow Skink	*Carlia rufilatus*	to 42mm
Striped Rainbow Skink	*Carlia munda*	to 44mm
Three-spined Rainbow Skink	*Carlia triacantha*	to 53mm

The most common small skinks, which rummage around in the leaf litter are the Rainbow skinks. The colour of most of them is usually a medium brown with variations of colour and intensity between species and increasing during breeding seasons. The distinguishing features are minor to the naked eye, and are best described by their common and scientific names. They are often seen bobbing their heads and waving their tails.

The Two-spined Rainbow Skink is uniformly brown with two fine keels on each scale (seen with a hand lens), and a very small white line under the eye. It is usually found in dry habitats.

The Slender Rainbow Skink is a very slender coppery brown skink found in open forest, woodland and open woodland, as well as along creeks and in closed forests as it prefers humid habitats. It is probably the most common Rainbow Skink in Darwin and town gardens, especially on compost heaps.

Two-spined Rainbow Skink, *Carlia amax*

Slender Rainbow Skink
Carlia gracilis

The Red-sided Rainbow Skink is most easily recognised by a rusty-red stripe along the sides. The Striped Rainbow Skink Carlia munda is distinguished by a white stripe along the lips, beyond the ear and along the side.

Red-sided Rainbow Skink *Carlia rufilatus*

The largest of the five Carlias in the region is the Three-spined Rainbow Skink. The spines refer to the fine striations on the surface of each scale, seen with a hand lens. This is the only one in the region with three.

The striped Rainbow Skink is distinguished by a white stripe along the lips beyond the ear and along the side. The colourful breeding males are territorial, and are attracted by the rustling of leaves, thinking it is an intruding male.

Striped Rainbow Skink *Carlia munda* in breeding colours

Three-spined Rainbow Skink
Carlia triacantha

Snake-eyed or Fire-tailed Skinks

Top End Firetail Skink *Morethia storri*   to 38mm
Lined Fire-Tailed Skink *Morethia ruficauda*   to 36mm

Morethia ruficauda   *Morethia storri*

Two small skinks, not so common in Darwin region commonly seen in Litchfield and Kakadu are the Fire-tailed or Snake-eyed skinks. At first they appear very similar, but are easily distinguished by the intensity of colour. The Fire-tailed Morethia is coloured black with four strong white stripes running from head to hind limbs, and has a bright red tail. Storr's Morethia is rich to light brown, with a dark lateral stripe separated from the back by a white mid-lateral stripe. The tail is pale reddish to brownish. Both inhabit drier habitats in open woodland, open forest, shrubland and coastal areas.

Tree Skink (Swanson's Snake-Eyed Skink) *Cryptoblepharus cygnatus*

Those very quick skinks, which run up and down trees, rails, fences and walls are almost certainly the Snake-eyed Skinks. The most common in the Darwin region grows to about 47 millimetres (SVL). The body is usually patterned with small black flecks over a grey, olive-grey or coppery brown ground colour. The Tree Skink has a flattened appearance, and 5 long fingers and toes. Found in most habitats in the region, it may also inhabit rocky outcrops. The skink in this photo is supplementing its diet with nectar from *Cordia subcordata.*

Stripy or Comb-eared Skinks *Ctenotus*

Australia's largest genus of reptiles is the 'comb-eared' ('cten-ot'-us) skink group *Ctenotus*, referring to the prominent ear lobules. They are most abundant in the arid zone and the seasonally dry tropics, and found only in Australia, and one species in New Guinea. The Darwin region is home to a number, some of which are very common. Most of the skinks in this genus are striped or have parallel series of spots or dashes along the body. All of these skinks have 5 fingers and toes.

Northern Ctenotus *Ctenotus borealis*

One of the largest in the region, the Northern Ctenotus is not very common, but is very distinctive when seen. It is a very fast lizard growing to 121 millimetres, with a long tapering tail and brown, fawn or olive-brown body. The Northern Ctenotus is found in a wide variety of dry habitats, from Pandanus-dominated grassy dunes to open savanna woodland, and rock outcrops. They shelter in burrows under rocks and ground cover.

Robust Ctenotus *Ctenotus robustus*

The Robust Ctenotus is about as robust as the Northern Ctenotus and about the same length (up to 123mm). It is also very fast. The main obvious differences are the stronger patterns. The Robust Ctenotus has a black vertebral stripe edged with white, and a series of stripes and dots running along the back and sides. It is much more common than the Northern Ctenotus, and is found in a wide variety of habitats, from sand dunes to woodlands and forests, and prefers thicker ground cover.

Plain Ctenotus *Ctenotus inornatus*

Plain is not a word that should be used with lizards. They are all richly coloured and patterned, some more so than others. The Plain Ctenotus is a fairly large (up to 95mm) skink coloured brown and patterned with dark and pale stripes along the back and sides. *Ctenotus inornatus* is abundant across the Top End and in the Kimberleys, commonly found in open habitat, particularly grassy flats and river banks, and in rocky outcrops and beach dunes.

The next group of Stripy Skinks or Ctenotus found in the region are smaller than the above three:

Storr's Ctenotus *Ctenotus storri*	40mm
Ten-lined Ctenotus *Ctenotus decaneurus*	50mm
Hill's Ctenotus *Ctenotus hilli*	50mm
Port Essington Ctenotus *Ctenotus essingtonii*	60mm

Storr's Ctenotus is a small skink with 8 simple pale stripes on a dark background. The Ten-lined Ctenotus usually has 10 pale vertebral stripes. Hill's Ctenotus has a complex pattern of stripes and spots, sometimes with a dark vertebral stripe. The Port Essington Ctenotus, first described from Port Essington on the Cobourg Peninsula in 1842, has either a complex or reduced pattern. They are all very similar in appearance, and take an expert to tell apart.

The Port Essington Ctenotus is common in the Darwin area, found in gardens and beach reserves and prefers open spaces. The Ten-lined Ctenotus is common on rocky microhabitats, whereas Hill's Ctenotus prefers lateritic uplands with stony surfaces, sheltering and foraging amongst grass tussocks, rocks, logs and leaf litter. Storr's Ctenotus is common and usually found in flat sandy habitats with grassy understorey, in sandy open forest.

Both Hills and Storr's Ctenotus are endemic to the north-west Arnhem region, which includes the Darwin area, whereas the other two are more widespread.

Dragons

Frill-necked Lizard *Chlamydosaurus kingii*

This king of dragons was named after Captain Phillip Parker King in 1825. It is found across northern Australia and in New Guinea, demonstrating the ancient land links between the two land masses. The large frill is a flap of skin erected by the lizard opening its jaws wide.

The Frill-necked Lizard grows to about 200 millimetres from snout to vent, with a tail that is about twice that length. It may display on roads and tracks. When disturbed it will run very fast on its hind legs to a tree (not always the nearest), and rapidly climb the hidden side to about breast height. It will keep the tree between predators such as humans and itself by moving around the tree for protection.

Gilberts Dragon *Lophognathus gilberti*
Tree Dragon *Gowidon temporalis*

These two dragons are very similar, both with nuchal crests along the spine which is continuous with a strong vertebral ridge, are fawn to reddish-brown above and pale beneath, and both with white stripes along the sides of their bodies. They grow up to 400 millimetres long (SVL), with tails 3 times as long as their bodies, and very long hind limbs.

These two dragons are most often found in trees in a range of habitats from coastal dunes to tropical woodlands and open forests and monsoon forests. *Gowidon temporalis* is usually found near paperbark swamps, lagoons, creeks and riverine vegetation. Gilberts Dragon is usually found in drier open habitats, perched on trees, termite mounds and logs, and also near streams and swamps.

JM

Lophognathus gilberti

Gowidon temporalis

Two-lined Dragon *Diporiphora bilineata*

The Two-lined Dragon has two lines along its upper body coloured white to yellow and varies from pale grey to brown or reddish brown, often with a pattern of darkish angular blotches between and across the stripes. It grows to about 50 millimetres, with a long tail about 2.3 times the length of the body. Usually found on the ground, this dragon will climb low vegetation and fallen timber. It is found in a variety of habitats from coastal sand dunes to open woodlands and forests and closed forests, and is quick.

White-lipped Dragon *Diporiphora albilabris*

A closely related species, the White-lipped Dragon is found in the drier areas of the north-west Northern Territory. It may have pale stripes similar to the Two-lined Dragon and is about the same length. The lips are whitish but not conspicuously so. It is found on the ground or among low vegetation in open woodlands, particularly in the more rocky habitats south of Darwin.

Geckoes

Window Lizards of Northern Australia

native

introduced

Northern Dtella
Gehyra australis

Asian House Gecko
Hemidactylus frenatus

Asian House Gecko *Hemidactylus frenatus*

The gecko most people will see in the Darwin region is the House Gecko, also known as the 'chik-chak' because of the frequent calls uttered in and around houses. Colouration is usually pale whitish and uniform. It is found across northern Australia, almost always associated with houses and humans. The gecko is introduced to Australia, naturally occurring in south-east Asia. It grows to about 60 millimetres, and easily loses its tail. At night it scampers over walls and windows, catching any insects that land. Fights and disputes are common between House Geckoes.

Northern Dtella *Gehyra australis*

Northern Dtellas are also found in houses and buildings, but appear to be replaced in most towns by the House Gecko. The House Gecko has claws on each toe, while the Northern Dtella is missing a claw on the inner toes of each foot. The Northern Dtella is about 70 millimetres long (SVL). The underbelly is translucent, and when carrying eggs, they can be seen as two white patches. The Northern Dtella is usually a pale to dark grey or grey-brown above. The colour, especially below, can vary with temperature and activity. Northern Dtellas are arboreal and live in a variety of woodlands and coastal and riverine forests, as well as buildings.

Bynoe's Prickly Gecko *Heteronotia binoei*

The small, slender Bynoe's Gecko has series of raised spots on its body and is often coloured dark brown with yellow pin points of colour, but is very variable. The raised spots and slender, birdlike feet and thin tail easily distinguish it. It grows to 50mm, and lives in a very wide variety of habitats, including on beach dunes, under cover.

Marbled Velvet Gecko *Oedura marmorata*

The strikingly-coloured Marbled Velvet Gecko grows to about 90mm, and may be coloured with yellow and brown patches, brown and yellow bands, or grey and white bands. Marbled Geckoes live in rocky habitats or in trees, under bark.

Zigzag velvet Gecko *Oedura rhombifer*

This distinctive gecko is rich brown above, with a long series of pale diamond-shaped markings along the spine. Growing to 70 millimetres, this Velvet Gecko is usually arboreal, and lives under loose bark. It is often found in man-made dumps and in buildings.

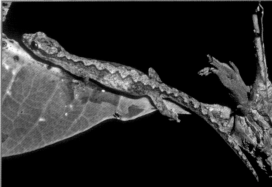

Northern spiny-tailed Gecko *Strophurus ciliaris*

This large gecko (90 mm) is easily identified by spines along the tail and above the eye. It is very variable in colour and can be quite bright. When touched, it can exude a sticky fluid from the base of the spines on the tail. The gecko is arboreal and found in a wide variety of habitats.

Varanids

Gould's Goanna
Varanus gouldii

Gould's Goanna is a very wide-spread goanna with a distinctive yellow tail end, and variably patterned body with black, yellow and ochre colours, but no transverse rows of large, dark spots. It is entirely terrestrial, living and foraging in logs, under rocks and amongst leaf litter. It is the largest goanna in the region, growing up to about 1.6 metres total length, and eats insects, live vertebrates and carrion.

Yellow spotted Monitor
Varanus panoptes

Panoptes Goanna was for a long time confused with Gould's Goanna. It differs by having numerous large spots on its back - Panoptes means 'all eyes' and was one of the names of Argus in Greek mythology, and by the dark tip to its tail. It grows to about 1.4 metres.

Spotted Tree Monitor

Yellow spotted monitor

Gould's Goanna

Varanus scalaris

This round-tailed Spotted Tree Monitor is usually grey to black above, with a series of white flecks. It lives in trees, hollow logs and under loose bark, and grows to 60cm total length, with a tail about 1.5 times as long as the body.

Freckled Monitor
Varanus tristis

The slightly larger (76 cm total length) Black-tailed Tree Monitor is black in McDonnell Ranges, otherwise freckled in the Top End.
Most of the tail is usually black, and may be 2.3 times as long as the body. It is usually arboreal, but may also live in rock crevices.

Spotted Tree Monitor

Freckled Monitor

Pygopods (Legless Lizards)

Northern Delma *Delma borea*

The fairly common Northern Delma or legless lizard usually has distinctive broad bands, broken by yellow lines across the head and neck. It is often mistaken for a snake, but is harmless. It grows to 80mm (snout-vent) and is found in a wide variety of habitats.

Burton's Snake-lizard *Lialis burtonis*

Burton's Snake-lizard is readily identified by its long, flat, wedge-shaped head. It can be quite variable in colour and grows to about 300 millimetres (SVL). It is found in a wide variety of habitats and is active day and night.

Snakes

Children's Python *Antaresia childreni*

Apparently named after the English naturalist John Children, the snake is well-named for its small size and mostly docile nature. The Children's Python is light to reddish brown, usually with faint bands across it body, and grows to about 85-95 centimetres total length. It is found in a variety of habitats, and is mostly terrestrial. It is harmless, and non-venomous.

Black-headed Python *Aspidites melanocephalus*

The head, neck and throat of this handsome python are shiny black, and the body is usually cross-banded with light to dark brown and reddish-brown or blackish bands. The belly is cream to yellow. It grows to 1.5 metres, although larger specimens are sometimes seen. It is found in a wide variety of habitats and eats vertebrates, including poisonous snakes. It is terrestrial and non-poisonous.

Olive Python *Liasis olivaceus*

The large (2.5 to 4 metres) Olive Python is usually immaculate olive-brown with cream belly. It lives in savanna woodland and monsoon forests, as well as rocky hills and ranges, and is mostly terrestrial. It eats mammals, birds and reptiles, catching them by waiting quietly along trails. Small wallabies may be taken. It is non-poisonous.

Carpet Python *Morelia spilota*

Carpet Pythons are very variable in colour, but typically pale to dark brown with blackish blotches, sometimes with pale centres. The lips are usually yellow with vertical black bands. They are often arboreal, but may also live on the ground, and are found in a very wide range of habitats. They grow to about 2 metres, but have been recorded up to 4 metres long. Non-poisonous, they eat terrestrial vertebrates.

Common Tree Snake *Dendrelaphis punctulata*

This agile, slender, tree snake, up to 1.2 – 1.4 metres long, is variable in colour from grey to olive-brown, to almost black, usually with a lemon-yellow belly. When aroused, it shows a light blue colour between the flattened scales. It inhabits woodlands, monsoon forests and open forests, sometimes seen in Pandanus. It eats frogs, birds, reptiles and small mammals. Non-venomous.

Brown Tree Snake *Boiga irregularis*

A broad-headed tree snake which is brown to bright reddish brown and often with cross-bands. It grows to 1.4 metres, but sometimes up to 2 metres, and is very aggressive when disturbed, striking accurately with open mouth. The Brown Tree Snake eats small mammals, birds, eggs, and lizards. It is a rear-fanged venomous snake, which is not regarded as dangerous to humans. Habitats are similar to the Common Tree Snake.

Greater black Whip Snake *Demansia papuensis*

VENOMOUS. This fast, dark olive-brown or black snake is usually found in drier habitats. It prefers to escape when disturbed, and grows to about 1.65 metres in total length. It feeds on small vertebrates, mostly lizards.

Western Brown Snake *Pseudonaja nuchalis*

DANGEROUS. This snake, which grows to 1.5 metres overall, varies in colour and pattern from light brown to almost black. It may have a black head and nape, and is fast and aggressive. It is found in a wide range of habitats, and feeds on small mammals and reptiles, and can be active day and night in the tropics.

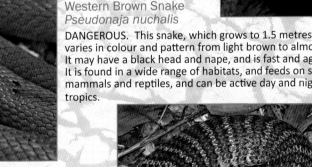

Northern Death Adder *Acanthophis praelongus*

DANGEROUS. A viper-like snake characterised by a broad, triangular head, narrow neck, short stout body to 70 centimetres, and thin rat-like tail ending in a curved soft spine. Its colour is grey to reddish-brown, often with cross-bands. Active at night, during the day they are found half-buried in sand, soil and litter. They attract prey, mammals and reptiles, by twitching the tip of the tail as a lure.

Mammals

More than 50 species of mammals inhabit the region around Darwin. Most are small, secretive and nocturnal. Larger ones such as Agile Wallabies and Antilopine Kangaroos are the most obvious, while some of the smaller ones, like the Northern Brown Bandicoot, Dusky Rat and Northern Quoll are regularly seen.

Northern Brown Bandicoot *Isoodon macrourus*

This common bandicoot is a large animal up to 470 millimetres and weighing in at up to 3.1 kilograms. Its brown body and pointy snout make it very identifiable. It lives in woodland, forest, and sometimes closed forest, preferring good shrub or ground cover. Insects, spiders and earthworms as well as berries, seeds and plants all form part of its diet. Scratchings and diggings in open areas indicate the presence of this bandicoot.

Northern Quoll *Dasyurus hallucatus*

The carnivorous Northern Quoll is the size of a small cat (up to 310mm), and is grey-brown above with white spots over its body. Its tail is hairy and unspotted. It is partly arboreal, and lives on small mammals, reptiles, insects and fruit. Due to Cane toads it is now uncommon in forests,woodlands and rocky areas.

Grassland Melomys *Melomys burtoni*

Living in dense vegetation, grasslands and woodlands with good grass understorey, as well as in monsoon forests, this rat is often cinnamon or khaki coloured. It grows to 130-140 millimetres, and eats grass stems, seeds and fruit. It has a scaly tail in a mosaic pattern, not like the overlapping concentric scales of other rats, and its tail is slightly prehensile. It can be locally abundant.

Antilopine Wallaroo *Macropus antilopinus*

One of the largest kangaroos in Australia, Antilopine Wallaroo males can grow to 1.2 metres from head to tail, and standing on their hind legs can be close to 2 metres tall. It prefers the open savanna woodlands and grasslands. It is gregarious, often seen in groups of 8 or more.

Agile Wallaby *Macropus agilis*

This small wallaby lives in the open forests and woodlands of the Top End. It is a fawny colour with a pale belly, and grows to about 60 - 80 centimetres head-body length. It has a pale stripe along the side of its face. It is often seen in mobs of 10 or so, sometimes more where food is good. It eats grasses, and is often seen in the Darwin area, such as at East Point, and also on the black soil floodplains during the dry season.

Northern Brushtail Possum
Trichosurus vulpecula

This feisty possum is found in the open forests and woodlands, and sometimes the houses of the region. It grows to about 42 centimetres, and has a sparsely bushy tail about 26 centimetres long. It is usually reddish-grey, and feeds on eucalypt leaves, supplemented with fruits, buds, bark and some other plants.

Sugar Glider
Petaurus breviceps

A handsome grey glider with a dark stripe down the middle of the back, and a cream belly, the Sugar Glider can sometimes be seen gliding from tree to tree in open forest, especially where the trees are tall and have plenty of hollows. They grow to about 20 centimetres (head-body), and have a long bushy tail about the same length. They eat acacia gum, eucalypt sap, and invertebrates.

Northern Blossom Bat *Macroglossus minimus*

The fur or pelage on this nectar and pollen-eating bat is brown to light brown, with reddish brown wings. It grows to 7 centimetres, and has no tail. The bat is relatively common in the Darwin region, often in monsoon forests, dense riverine vegetation, and mangroves. It is regularly seen in Darwin Botanic Gardens, feeding on the blossoms of the introduced Sausage tree Kigelia pinnata.

Dusky Horseshoe Bat *Hipposideros ater*

The pelage on this bat is light to mid-brown and it grows to about 5 centimetres, and has a tail of about 2.5 centimetres. It lives in caves during the day, and at night flies with a slow and very maneuverable flight. It can be locally common, and forages for insects in dense vegetation close to the ground.

Northern Blossom Bat   Dusky Horseshoe Bat   Sugar Glider

Some of the butterflies and caterpillars of the Top End and Darwin region

Common Crow *Euphloea core*

Common Crow caterpillar *Euphloea core*

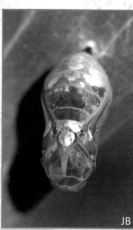

Common Crow chrysalis

Two-brand Crows *Euploea sylvester* on *Crotalaria*

Common Eggfly *Hypolimnas bolina*

Lesser Wanderer *Danaus petilla*

Swamp Tiger *Danaus affinis*

Tawny Coster, *Acrea,* a newly self introduced butterfly to Australia from south-east Asia. It also occurs in South Africa. It seems to be displacing Acerea on Hybanthus in NT

Blue Tiger *Tirumala hamata* (both photos)

Big Greasy *Cressida cressida*

Jezebel *Delias aestiva*

Orange Lacewing *Cethosia*

Fuscus Swallowtail *Papilio fuscus*

Blue Argus *Junonia orithya*

Lemon Migrants *Catopsilia*

Glasswing and caterpillars
Acraea andromacha

Grass Yellows & chrysalis
Eurema hecabe

Glasswing *Acraea andromacha* pupae being carried by Green Tree Ants

Some of the moths and caterpillars of the Top End and Darwin region

Four o'clock Moth *Dysphanea numana*

Four o'clock Moth caterpillar

Atlas Moth *Attacus wardi* endemic to NT

Atlas Moth caterpillar

Fruit Piercing Moths

family

Noctuidae

Eudocima salaminia *Othreis materna*

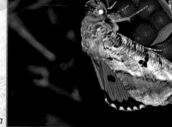

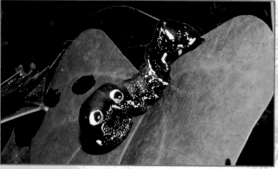
Fruit Piercing Moth caterpillar

Fruit Piercing Moth caterpillar

Bag Moth caterpillars *Ochrogaster lunifera* family Notodontidae

Bag Moths are communal caterpillars. They climb the Cocky Apple, Planchonia caraya tree in the night to eat the leaves. During the day they sleep in their bag. In the bag their protruding spines protect them from predators. When they finish stripping the leaves of one tree they climb down and move to another tree.

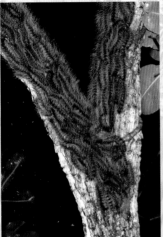

Emperor Moths
family Saturniidae

Sytherata melvilla
Occurs in varying coloured morphs, as seen in the 2 photos below.

family Noctuidae

Erebus sp.   *Speiredonia sp.*

Hawk Moths and caterpillars family Sphingidae

Theretra inornata   *Daphnis hypothous moorei*   *Theretra indistincta*   *Cephonodes picus*

Cup Moths and larvae family Limacodidae

Cup Moth larvae spines burn your skin

CHAPTER SIX

Monsoon Forests

Our monsoon forests are time capsules from when rainforests were once widespread across a wetter northern Australia (see *Chapter 2*). Today, rainforest vegetation - more appropriately called monsoon vine forests, to acknowledge the influence of the strongly monsoonal climate - occurs in very small, widely separated patches. These patches occur in a variety of habitats from situations with year round water availability, to seasonally arid sites such as inland rocky outcrops and coastal beach ridges.

Buttress roots of Syzygium nervosum in a wet monsoon forest

Reflecting the variable moisture content of their soils, the monsoon forests range from dense, spring-fed, evergreen forests 20 to 30 metres high, to scrubby, but often floristically diverse semi-deciduous or deciduous vine forests and thickets in seasonally dry sites. In windswept coastal situations the canopy of these plant communities may be as low as 2 metres.

Evergreen Monsoon Vine Forests

Sites with perennially high soil moisture and reasonably good soil aeration develop evergreen forests characterised by a closed canopy and an abundance of broadleaved species. These 'jungles' have a high diversity of plant species, and where the dominant species often vary depending on the particular location. Palms and ferns find suitable conditions for growth in the moist shady understorey and abundant vines and climbers grow from underground tubers or yams, which are also an important food source for Aboriginal people. Holmes jungle in Darwin is a good example of one evergreen monsoon vine forest, in the Top End. We have provided information to this locality in Part 3.

In Litchfield, Katherine region, Kakadu, Arnhem Land, numerous springs can be found as examples of lushTop End jungles. Commonly observed plant species in jungles associated with permanent streams and perennial water include:

Cheeky Yam *Amorphophallus paeoniifolius*

An unusual herb growing to 1.5 m, with a fleshy, rough stem mottled in green and white, topped with very large, deeply divided leaves. Mature plants produce an odd looking flower first, before the leaves appear. The flower is a red-purple bract - a central column with numerous small flowers attached - and a weird, 40 cm, bladderlike structure. Flowers produce an unpleasant smell. Aboriginal people eat the roots of this species after extensive preparation. They describe it as 'cheeky' because it is poisonous; only yams that produce a clear sap are eaten. A white latex or white-flecked sap indicates that it is unsuitable to eat.

Calophyllum sil

A spreading, evergreen tree, with dark grey to black bark and distinctive glossy leaves, forming a dense, shade-casting, crown, commonly found on creek banks but extending to rocky areas. This species can grow to 20 m tall but more commonly to 12 m. The opposite leaves are elongated and oval with numerous small parallel veins and a prominent raised midrib beneath the leaf. Flowers are white, scented, held on short stalks at the base of the leaves during April to July. Fruits, to 2 cm, are round and smooth, and dark purple-black when ripe. This species may be confused with the similar Beauty Leaf, *Calophyllum inophyllum*, found on coastal cliffs and widely grown in cultivation, which has broader leaves and larger fruits, to 4 cm. Another species, *Calophyllum soulattri*, found only in moist jungles, can be distinguished from *C. sil* by its yellowish bark, longer leaves and long flower stalks. Holmes Jungle is the only site near Darwin where *Calophyllum soulattri* is found.

Carallia brachiata

A low to medium height evergreen tree with spreading layered branches, common throughout South East Asia. A common species found in many situations from the banks of freshwater streams to rocky sandstone outcrops. A relative of mangroves, *Carallia* is quite mangrove-like in appearance, with glossy, opposite, oval leaves with new leaves rolled to a point. Bark is pale, cream to grey coloured and corky. Very small, cream to green coloured flowers are produced in clusters in the leaf axils from July to October. The single-seeded berries are bright red when ripe and form during September to November. The timber has a variety of Aboriginal uses including spear shafts, spear heads, axe handles and music sticks.

Cyclophyllum schultzii

A shrub to small tree, 2 to 10 m high, that can be multi-stemmed, the trunks having smooth, tight dark grey bark. The leaves are opposite, narrow to broadly oval and 8-14 cm long. The highly fragrant flowers are held in clusters of 4 to 6 in the leaf axils. They are white but turn yellow with age, have 5-6 star like petals and feathery stamens. Fruits are 2-lobed, thin-fleshed, drupes about 1.5 cm across, eaten when soft and bright red, contain a pair of seeds. Favouring the sandy banks of streams and monsoon forest in lowland and sandstone areas.

Carpentaria Palm *Carpentaria acuminata*

Endemic to the northern regions of the Top End, the Carpentaria Palm is a hardy, fast growing palm that is widely grown in cultivation. A tall, single-stemmed palm with feather-type fronds 15-30 m high with a slender trunk to 15 cm diameter. The bark is smooth and cream-grey colour and ringed from old leaf bases. The fronds are dark green, evenly divided into leaflets with an arching growth form. Flowers are produced in large bunches on branching stalks just below the leaf stalk which sheaths the trunk. Male and female flowers form in separate bunches during September to December, followed by a profusion of rounded bright red fruits to 2 cm in diameter. The flowers and fruit of the Carpentaria palm represent an important resource for nectivorous and frugivorous birds.

Diospyros calycantha

One of several *Diospyros* species in the Top End, *D. calycantha* is a small, slender tree growing to 8 m. The bark is dark brown to black becoming tessellated on older trees. The alternate leaves are leathery, 6-12 cm long with distinct veins, a pointed tip and a stout leaf stalk. The oval leaves characteristically exhibit circular shaped dead patches, differentiating this species from other Diospyros species that occur in monsoon forest. The small white flowers are borne in the leaf axils during the wet season. Female flowers develop into a globular fruit up to 3 cm in diameter, orange-red when ripe. Each fruit has four prominent reflexed calyx lobes at the base - these persistent lobes are a good diagnostic feature. Ebony timber is derived from trees in the genus *Diospyros*.

Fagraea racemosa

A very attractive, small evergreen tree 4 to 10 m tall, commonly found on the banks of permanent freshwater streams. The slender trunk has slightly rough bark, grey to brown in colour. *Fagraea* has large, leathery, rounded leaves held on slender pendulous stalks. The highly fragrant white flowers are large and bell-shaped and held on drooping stalks at the ends of the branches. Fruits are smooth, green berries, ovoid in shape with a small pointed tip containing numerous small seeds.

Banyan or Strangler Fig *Ficus virens*

A large to extremely large spreading fig tree 15 to 30 m tall with entwining aerial roots. The banyan is a strangler fig, germinating in the fork of a host tree and gradually enveloping the tree and killing it. The bark is smooth and light grey and the tree characteristically has numerous aerial roots, which grow down from its spreading branches and become established as prop roots away from the main trunk of the tree. The leaves are ovate, smooth, not particularly thick, and the stems contain white latex. The tree is deciduous and may drop all its leaves and refoliate again within the space of a few days. Small, 1 cm, smooth-skinned greenish-white figs are produced sporadically but most often in the dry season. Aboriginal usage of the tree included string manufacture from the bark of aerial roots. The figs are edible. Often found in monsoon forests, on coastal cliffs and vine forests throughout the Top End.

Ficus hispida;

A small tree, 4 to 10 m high, common in the understorey layer of monsoon forests, typically in moist, heavy soils. This fig has male and female trees and is conspicuous for its large, coarsely hairy, opposite leaves. The stems are usually hollow and like other figs contain white latex. Flowers and fruit are flattened figs, yellow when ripe, borne on long drooping stems from the trunk and larger branches.

Cluster Fig *Ficus racemosa*

A tree to 15 m high with an open spreading canopy and smooth, pale grey bark. The trunk is typically buttressed at the base. The oval leaves are large 7 to 22 cm long with a pointed tip. Leaf venation is prominent and the stems contain a white latex. Noticeable for its large clusters of colourful figs that are produced on thick stalks arising from the lower branches the trunk of the tree. Most abundant during the dry season, the figs are 2 to 4 cm in diameter. Young figs are furry and green becoming smooth and yellow to reddish when ripe. Ripe figs are edible and a well documented Aboriginal food source, however they are dry and disappointing in comparison with cultivated fig varieties.

Flagellaria indica

A substantial vine, which may climb high into the canopy, forming smooth tough canes to 1.5 cm diameter. The alternate leaves are stem-clasping and a shiny bright green. The leaf tips curl up into a fine tendril which enables the vine to climb. Clusters of white, scented flowers, up to 10 cm long, are produced in terminal clusters. Flowers develop into small edible fruits that are whitish to orange-brown when ripe. The fibrous stems traditionally were prepared to make thread to sew Aboriginal baskets and fish traps, and woven to make body ornaments.

Hydriastele Palm *Hydriastele wendlandiana*

A multi-stemmed palm, endemic to the Top End. Slender green trunks ringed by old leaf bases grow to 15 m tall under favourable conditions. Fronds are feather-like with uneven-sized leaflets on a curved rachis. The leaflets are broadest in the middle and at the end of the frond with the terminal leaflets fused into a bow-like pair. Flowers and bright red fruit are produced in a drooping skirt that encircles the trunk just below the crown. Hydriastele palms are restricted to moist organic soils in monsoon forests and riverine habitats associated with permanent streams.

Climbing Maidenhair Fern *Lygodium flexuosum*

A common and widespread perennial climbing fern with slender twining stems. Delicate maidenhair-type leaves with variable shaped leaflets may be ovate to elongated. Spores borne on smaller fertile leaflets with very divided leaf margins. Climbs on trees and rocks and over vegetation in monsoon forests surrounding permanent streams, and around seepage zones in rocky areas.

Maranthes corymbosa

One of the larger evergreen trees of local monsoon forests, reaching 25 m high. Bark is rough grey-brown and slightly tessellated and the tree has a spreading, drooping habit. Young leaves may be covered with soft white hairs which disappear from older foliage which is shiny above and pale beneath. Leaves are elliptic, alternately arranged and held on very short stalks. Bunches of showy pale yellow flowers are produced in bunches at the ends of the branches during May to September. Fruit is a large ovoid berry, to 3 cm, containing a single woody seed. Berries turn from green to purple-black as they ripen. *Maranthes* has become a popular street tree around Darwin, with avenue plantings of young trees gracing Dick Ward Drive and Vanderlin Drive.

Livistona benthamii

Livistona benthamii is the only large, 18 m, fan palm in monsoon forests in the Darwin region. In suitable habitats it often forms single-species stands. The trunk may be up to 40 cm in diameter, and characteristically has persistent leaf bases, attached to the base of the trunk. Leaves are broad, fan shaped and convoluted with many deeply divided lobes. They are held on long stalks with numerous stout prickles along the edges. The palm flowers during May to August with numerous small white flowers on spikes up to 2 m long held upright within the canopy of the palm. Fruit are small round berries to 1 cm containing a single hard-shelled black seed. Found in habitats where there is permanent freshwater. Local occurrences of this species can be seen at Holmes Jungle, Howard Springs, Katherine and Mataranka.

Melicope elleryana

A slender, open-branched tree 10 to 20 m high with cream somewhat corky and crumbly bark. The opposite, glossy leaves are composed of three separate leaflets, the central leaflet being the largest, 9-20 cm long. The tiny, 5 mm, sweetly scented pink flowers are borne in dense upright clusters, to 10 cm wide, along the horizontal twigs and branches during November and December. Fruits are roundish leathery capsules turning from green to brown when ripe, at which time the fruit splits open, releasing a single shiny black seed. Melicope is an important food source for native animals, including butterflies and birds (especially the Red-collared Lorikeets) who enjoy the nectar-rich flowers. The seeds are a favourite food for possums and birds.

Nephrolepis biserrata

A robust, large fern growing to over 2 m high. Fronds are arched and upright with pinnate leaf formation where numerous leaflets branch out from the central stem. The leaf margins may be toothed and the individual leaflets may be

Black Flying Fox in Melicope

curved. Some fronds are fertile and the underside of the leaves have rows of circular sori or small structures containing spores or seeds. This fern is common in moist monsoon forests, swampy areas and on streambanks. It may colonise large areas spreading via its numerous runners.

Wild Passionfruit
Passiflora foetida

A climbing vine with thin, hairy, stems and tendrils commonly found on the fringes of monsoon forests and in disturbed areas. Pale green to yellow-green, 3-lobed leaves, 7 cm, are also covered with fine hairs. Lilac and white coloured passionfruit flowers with complex finely divided petals develop into fruits up to 2 cm in diameter. Only eat ripe yellow fruits, green fruits highly toxic. This species is a native to South America but is now widespread throughout the Top End and Northern Australia.

Climbing Fern Stenochlaena palustris

A second common tree-climbing species found in monsoon forests is Stenochlaena. Its mature leaves are coarse, large and have toothed margins - not very reminiscent of ferns as a rule, but its soft, furled, pinkish juvenile leaves are more characteristic of the group. Two types of leaf occur; abundant sterile leaves are stiff, shiny, up to 1 m long and broadly divided into leaflets. Fertile fronds are infrequently produced, have much narrower leaflets, and the spores are produced on the lower leaf surface. Green stems produce numerous adventitious roots, and the plant readily climbs over rocks and up tree trunks, or forms a tangled ground cover.

Smilax australis

A very common rambling climber found in monsoon forest and coastal vine-thicket habitats, often first noticed for its sharp, intermittently spaced thorns. Stems are green and smooth and up to 0.5 cm in diameter. Smilax climbs over other plants with the aid of wiry tendrils, and may climb many metres high. At the base of the stems are a number of conspicuous bracts. The oval leaves are variable in shape and size but are glossy above, alternately arranged, leathery and broad, with 3-5 prominent longitudinal veins which may give the leaf a pre-folded look. During November to March, ball-shaped clusters of greenish white, slightly fragrant flowers are produced on long stalks - the smaller female flowers are produced on separate plants from the male flowers. Inflorescences later develop small berries, to 1 cm, that are dark purple to black when mature. The fruit is edible when ripe. A treatment from the stem was made for sore eyes. The wood from the stems is also used as firesticks.

Sterculia holtzei

A tall, straight, smooth trunked tree, 10 to 20 m high found in dense monsoon forest, commonly on stream banks. The bark is pale grey and often mottled and the base of the tree is typically buttressed. The leaves are broadly elliptic to ovate and occasionally heart-shaped. Each leaf has a long stalk, 2 to 9 cm long and the foliage is clustered to the ends of the branches. Flowering occurs from May to September when the small green-yellow urn-like flowers are produced in the leaf axils. The yellow banana-shaped fruit capsules are held in groups of four. When ripe, the strongly curved upper margin splits open to release the shiny black seeds. This species occurs in the Top End and the Kimberley and is a common canopy tree in the monsoon forest patches in the local Darwin region.

Syzygium armstrongii

A moderate to large evergreen tree with tight, relatively smooth, pale grey bark. The crown of leathery, opposite leaves is dense, and the tree has an overall upright (rather than spreading) habit. Leaves taper at both ends, have a pointed tip, distinct midrib and are about 10 cm long, and distinctly shiny. Flowering occurs in September to December when dense branching clusters of 1-1.5 cm white flowers form a showy display. The white fruits have a single seed enclosed in a spongy, wrinkled, edible coating. Dugout canoes were made from the wood.

Syzygium minutuliflorum

A tree 15 to 25 m high, with dense foliage and flaky, creamy-brown bark. Larger trees may have a buttressed trunk. The somewhat oval leaves are opposite, smooth and leathery 7 to 12 cm long with a rounded tip. The leaves are a rich dark green above and paler with a raised midrib beneath. The white flowers are about 1 cm across and have numerous stamen. The small white fruits are pear-shaped, fleshy and only 1 to 2 cm in diameter, readily distinguishing this species from other local Syzygiums with larger fruits. The fruits are edible and float in water which assists their dispersal through riverine habitats. This species is endemic to the Top End but is restricted to habitats with ample soil moisture, such as the permanent springs and streams at Petherick's Rainforest.

Syzygium nervosum

Capable of growing to a very large tree, to 25 m, where there is ample soil moisture, this species has a broad crown of dense evergreen foliage. The bark is rough, dark cream to grey-brown and becoming flaky. Leaves are opposite, smooth and leathery, 10-18 cm long, and the edges are often wavy. Flowers are typical of Syzygiums being cream with numerous stamens produced in showy clusters. Flowering occurs during September to November. The fruits are oval 1-1.5 cm diameter, with a slightly depressed apex, dark purple to black when ripe. Prefers habitats with permanent ground water supply and swampy to heavy wet black soils. Fine examples are found at Berry Springs and Howard Springs Nature Parks. It is widely distributed through Northern Australia, Indonesia, China and India.

Terminalia microcarpa

A large spreading tree, to 30m high, often with a buttressed trunk. A distinctive layered appearance from spreading horizontal branches is a feature. One of the dominant tree species in monsoon forest patches in the Darwin Area. It has rough, dark grey to black bark which is often longitudinally fissured. Variable in shape, the leaves are spirally arranged, oval and shiny above, paler beneath. The tree drops its leaves for a short time during the late dry season. The leaves may turn a bright red before being shed. The tree produces a profusion of strong, rather unpleasant smelling flowers during September to November. The ovoid fruits are thinly fleshed, red to purple when ripe, and a favourite among frugivorous birds and mammals. The fruits are sweet and are excellent bush tucker.

Snake Vine Tinospora smilacina

A widespread woody climber with smooth stems of young vines becoming grey and corky with age. The triangular or heart-shaped leaves are 5 to 10 cm long, are alternately arranged, and are a glossy green. Plants in drier sites are semi-deciduous. Cream flowers, about 0.5 cm, are clustered on stalks 15 cm long, appearing during the dry season. Red fruits to 1 cm contain ornately sculptured brown seeds. Twining stems can make their way to the canopy of forest trees and the corky stems of very old plants may reach 10 cm in diameter. Vines of these dimensions may outlive or even strangle their host trees.

Vavaea australiana

Generally a slender tree to 10 m with a layered branching habit and with leaves held in clusters toward the end of the branches. Flowers are held in clusters of 5 to 20 and are produced on longish stalks from August to January. Individual blooms are white and star-shaped, have 5 to 6 petals and are sweetly scented. Orange rounded berries containing up to 4 seeds become shiny and black when ripe, and form continuously while the tree is flowering. *Vavaea*, like many monsoon forest species, is widely distributed through Indonesia and some of the Pacific Islands. Its name, 'Vavaea' refers to the island of Vavua, Tonga.

Xanthostemon eucalyptoides

A tall spreading tree to 20 m high commonly found along the banks of creeks, springs and water bodies fringed with monsoon forest. The grey bark is fibrous and flaky. The broad, oblong leaves are stalkless, arranged opposite one another and clustered toward the end of the branches. cvFlowering occurs between July and October, and like the Eucalypts that also occur in the same botanical family (Myrtaceae), flowers have numerous stamens on a shallow basal cup. Individual flowers are fused in roundish terminal clusters, 3 - 7 cm across, and are a rich source of nectar for birds and insects. Fine wafer-like seeds are contained in round, woody capsules which split into 3 to 4 segments when ripe. See also *Xanthostemon paradoxus*, a similar yellow-flowering species from the woodland habitat.

A locally endangered jungle palm

Ptychosperma macarthurii

Ptychosperma macarthurii is an endangered palm species which occurs only in very small populations near Darwin. The palm is associated with springs bubbling from the upland margin of the Adelaide River floodplain. The palm prefers sandy loam soils and good soaking each year with the monsoons. The palm grows to 10-12 m and flowers and seeds annually. In experimental conditions these seeds germinate after 3-6 months. Given this, it is disturbing to discover that the species is declining. The severe detrimental effect of late season wildfires that engulf monsoon pockets, and the effects of disturbance and feral animals are taking their toll on this endangered plant species of the Top End.

Perhaps because of its close proximity to Darwin, considerable efforts have been made to conserve the remaining populations. For instance, populations of *P. macarthurii* were included in the Black Jungle Reserve in March 1986, populations on cattle stations have been fenced, and a recovery plan has been drawn up.

Deciduous Monsoon Vine Forests

These monsoon forests are not associated with perennial supplies of water. Growing on coastal cliffs, amongst sand dunes, and inland on rock outcrops, they become dry toward the end of the dry season. Most species survive by progressively dropping their leaves or by retaining them in a wilted state. Depending on the degree of leaf-shed this vegetation is termed semi-deciduous or deciduous monsoon vine forest.

Good examples of semi-deciduous vine forest can be seen along the Kadadu highway, Stuart Highway near and beyond Katherine, and in the Darwin region along Casuarina Coastal Reserve and East Point. The canopy is typically less than 10metres high and is often covered by a tangle of vines.

Field guide to Coastal Vine Forest species

Crabs Eye Vine *Abrus precatorius*

A slender, perennial vine commonly found entwining other coastal vine forest species, it develops a woody stem with age. It is deciduous, losing its leaves during the dry season. The foliage is fine (the name Abrus means delicate), with compound leaves divided into 8 to 16 pairs of leaflets, up to 2 cm long. The vine produces pink-mauve peaflowers during January to April. The pods are flat and woody and contain highly poisonous seeds which are bright red with a black spot at one end. The seeds may remain on the vine for a long time after the pods ripen. The species name precatorius means praying and refers to their having been used as rosary beads.

Darwin black wattle *Acacia auriculiformis*

A large tree, with a dense, spreading canopy commonly 10 to 20 metres high, and rough, dark brown to black, fissured bark; a common and widespread species in coastal and lowland monsoon vine forests. Like several other Acacia species it is drought tolerant, hardy and an effective coloniser, particularly of disturbed coastal jungles (for example after fires, cyclones). The 'leaves' are phyllodes or expanded stems, curved, elongated and of variable size but typically 10 to 17 cm long. Flowering occurs in the mid dry season, May to July, when the tree is covered in a profusion of yellow, heavily fragrant cylindrical spikes. Leathery seed pods are curled and twisted, ear shaped and up to 7 cm long.

Aidia racemosa

A slender tree 5 to 15 m high with a layered branching habit . The bark is smooth and grey, often with a blotchy appearance. The opposite, glossy leaves are smooth and elongated, with distinct venation and tapering to a pointed tip.. The leaves are held close to the branches on very short stalks. The white flowers are highly scented and showy. Flowers are held in raised clusters above the branches during August to December. Individual flowers have a prominent protruding style and later develop into bright red berries. The berries are up to 1 cm across and held in clusters of 20 and contain several small seeds. Aboriginal people used the wood for making spear shafts.

Canarium australianum

A shapely, deciduous, tree with a rounded crown to 25 m high, common in coastal vine-thickets. Bark is cream to grey and smooth and slightly scaly. The large compound leaves, up to 30 cm long, are composed of up to 7 oblong leaflets. The upper leaf surface is smooth, and the undersurface typically finely hairy. The leaf margins are finely serrated. Male and female flowers are produced on separate trees. The deep red flowers form on spikes in the leaf axils. Female trees form oval shaped fruits, about 1.5 cm, during September to December. These are blue-black and edible when ripe. They contain a single hard seed. Aboriginal people use this species for a variety of medicinal purposes including bark infusions for diarrhoea, and leaf and fruit preparation to stop bleeding after childbirth.

Celtis philippensis

A pantropical, hardy, semi-deciduous slender tree to 7 m, occasionally taller, with smooth bark a mottled cream to grey colour, common in vine-thickets in harsh sites. On inland rock outcrops, it may be one of few species to retain its leaves during the dry. The stiff leaves are alternate, brittle and ovate, forming a dense rounded crown. Each leaf has 3 prominent longitudinal veins and a pointed tip. Juvenile leaves have toothed edges. Small, inconspicuous flowers form during October to December and fruits are globular, slightly flattened and fleshy and bright red when ripe. Aboriginal people eat the raw fruits.

Drypetes deplanchei

A small, fairly compact semi-deciduous tree usually 5 to 7 m tall. The characteristic light grey bark is tight, smooth and blotchy - often supporting encrusting lichens. Juvenile leaves are holly-like with sharp-toothed margins. Adult leaves are extremely variable in shape and size - being oval to elongated, with the tip indented to pointed. Generally leaves are tough, leathery, paler beneath and alternately arranged. Male and female trees produce insignificant creamy-green inflorescences on short stalks. The red fleshy fruits are oval to 2cm long and ripen during the wet season. They are edible. The juice produces a strong dark dye. Other Aboriginal uses include carving utensils from the wood.

Elaeocarpus arnhemicus

A small to moderate-sized tree 5 to 15 m high with dense, compact foliage and smooth grey bark. The glossy leaves are alternate, oval and 5 to 11 cm long with bluntly serrated margins and long pointed tips. During March to August very small white flowers form on stalks up to 8 cm long. In fruit, this species is most outstanding - producing a striking crop of bright blue fruit clustered in the leaf axils. Each fruit encloses a hard, pitted nut. A hardy evergreen species occurring in both deciduous vine-thickets in coastal situations and in monsoon forests associated with permanent water. Aboriginal uses of the plant include making canoes from the wood and the ripe fruit is edible. The fruit is also favoured by birds, especially pigeons

Native jasmine Jasminum aemulum

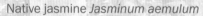

A scrambling shrub 3 to 4 m high, or vigorous woody climber twining through other foliage to 15 m high. The leaves are opposite, smooth and trifoliate (composed of three leaflets) the central leaflet being the largest, 3 to 10 cm long. Each leaflet is shiny green and distinctly veined, with raised venation beneath. The flowers have a sweet, pungent scent. Individual flowers are white, about 1 cm x 1 cm and held in showy branching clusters usually at the ends of the branches. Blue-black berries about 1 cm in diameter contain the single seeds.

Rotten Cheesefruit Morinda citrifolia

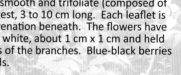

A small, semi-deciduous tree to 8 m with dense foliage common around the Top End foreshore. The glossy, opposite leaves are relatively large at 10-30 cm long. Elliptical leaves have wavy margins, prominent venation and a pointed tip. The flowers are odd-looking, with small, white flowers appearing sequentially on globular fleshy green heads. Individual fruits are fused into a composite fleshy mass that swells to the size of a pear, turning from green to white when ripe. The squashy ripe fruits contain numerous brown seeds embedded in odorous pulp, which is edible. Fruit preparations are used to treat colds, flu and diarrhoea. An infusion from the leaves is also a treatment for diarrhoea. A yellow dye is obtained from the roots, and used for dying baskets

Pouteria sericea

A small, straggly tree 3 to 10 m tall with rough, light to dark grey bark, often finely fissured. The leaves are distinctive, being dull, dark green and smooth above, but covered with silky, rusty, golden hairs beneath. The leaf tip is indented and the stalk is short and usually hairy. The foliage is crowded along the stems and often insect-eaten and untidy looking. Flowers are small, pale green to white, scented and narrowly tubular. The edible fruits are smooth, ovoid and a shiny purple black when ripe. They are sweet, and have been likened to a date in flavour. A widespread species most common in coastal semi-deciduous monsoon vine forest and thicket.

Gyrocarpus americanus

A thick-trunked deciduous tree, 6 to 12 m high, with generally crooked branches, and outstanding silvery-bronze smooth bark, common in semi-deciduous vine forest. The alternate leaves are variably shaped, from heart-shaped to 3 or 5 lobed. Leaves are sparsely hairy, with distinct venation and long stalks. Flowers are tiny, cream coloured, and held in tight clusters in branching inflorescences. The unusual two-winged fruits give the tree its name; *Gyrocarpus* refers to the way the fruits gyrate or whirl when falling from the tree; carpus means fruit. Mature seeds often remain attached to the tree for several months. Popularly known as 'helicopter trees' by Darwin children, it's always worth giving these trees a good shake - no matter how old you are.

Peanut tree *Sterculia quadrifida*

A spreading tree generally, 5 to 10 m tall, hardy and deciduous, with smooth light grey bark, commonly found in coastal sites, but also inland on rocky outcrops. The broad, open crown has ovate to heart-shaped leaves, 9 to 20 cm long, with a pointed tip and slightly hairy undersurface. Flowers develop at the ends of the branches, and are greeny-yellow, 4-petalled with several bell-shaped blooms held on each stalk. The oval, leathery fruit capsules are often in pairs. These pods are bright red when ripe, splitting open to form boat shaped capsules containing 2 to 4 shiny black seeds. The peeled seeds have a peanut-like flavour, and are excellent bush tucker. Traditionally, the plant was also harvested for the inner bark, to make string, rope, nets and fishing lines. Leaves are used in cooking, and applied to wounds and stings. *Sterculia quadrifida* is a hardy deciduous species common in coastal vine thickets and forests, also found along coastal cliffs and dunes in the Top End region.

Tamarind *Tamarindus indica*

A large spreading tree 15-25 m high with a dense evergreen canopy. The distinctive bark is rough, grey-brown with longitudinal fissures. The pinnate leaves are composed of numerous very fine leaflets 5-26 mm long which are blue-green on the upper surface and slightly paler beneath. The tree develops a heavily branched canopy which casts dense shade. The pale yellow flowers have brownish yellow markings which give them an orchid-like appearance. Flowering occurs in greatest abundance during November to February. They have a slight perfume, which is strongest during the evening. The brown pods to 9 cm long are flattened, often twisted and contain an acidic, fibrous pulp that is edible. The tamarind tree is indigenous to Africa but is now widespread in the tropics where it is cultivated or naturalised in many countries. Introduced to the north Australian coast by the Macassans, tamarinds are scattered in coastal localities in vine thickets.

Wrightia pubescens

A small, common and widely distributed, semi-deciduous tree, generally 3 to 7 m high, with distinctive, tight, slightly rough, grey bark speckled with white spots. White sap is present in the stems. The opposite leaves are oblong, have a pointed tip and are softly hairy (thus the name 'pubescens' which means downy with soft hair). The scented white flowers are 2-3 cm across and have 5 twisted petals. Fruits are a surprisingly large cylindrical woody pod up to 25 cm long. Covered with small white flecks, the dark green fruit splits open when ripe to release the numerous feathery, plumed seeds. In the Darwin region it occurs at East Point, Casuarina coastal reserve and Channel Island.

Monsoon Forests on the rocks

Monsoon forests on rock outcrops occur in inland locations, such as on Mount Bundey near the Adelaide River, on a variety of rock types including basalts and granites, limestones and sandstones. Most of the species are deciduous.

Allophylus cobbe

A small tree or shrub with smooth grey bark. This species may be easily recognised by its compound leaves composed of 3 lobes. Each leaflet is thin-walled, has a toothed margin, is darker above than below, with the central leaflet being the largest from 4 to 13 cm long. Flowers are on slender spikes, and are small and geenish. They develop into small, fleshy red fruits to 7 mm diameter.

Monsoon vine thicket growing on granite hills, Mt Bundey

Rock Fig *Ficus platypoda*

Typically a small, spreading tree, to 6 m high, with an extensive system of clinging and aerial roots that run over and throughout adjacent rock crevices. Rock figs have smooth, pale grey bark, and thick alternate leaves which are characteristically hairy. The upper leaf surface is finely hairy, and the lower leaf surface more so. The flowers are contained within the inner wall of the fig, which are around 1 cm in diameter and pink-red to purple when ripe. In reality the fig is the fleshy swollen end of the stem surrounding the flowers.

Grewia brevifolia

A deciduous multi-stemmed shrub or small tree, 3 to 8 m high, *Grewia* is a common species in rocky vine thickets. The mottled grey bark is smooth to slightly rough. Alternate, coarsely hairy leaves are held on spreading branches. The elongated, serrated leaves have three distinct longitudinal veins. Flowers appear in October-December, are rounded, yellow-orange in colour and held in small clusters. Seeds are contained in 1 or 2-lobed usually hairy, flattened fruits. Edible purple-black tasty fruit.

Strychnine tree *Strychnos lucida*

A small spreading tree, usually 2 to 5 m tall, with a rounded crown and drooping branchlets. The trunk has smooth blotchy, pale grey bark. Leaves are oppositely arranged, oval and discolorous - the upper surface a shiny dark green and the lower surface much paler. The 3 prominent leaf veins are a characteristic feature of the species. During October to January, perfumed tubular flowers are produced in dense terminal clusters of up to 30 flowers. The fruits are thin-walled, bright orange berries 3-4 cm in diameter, and contain a pulp in which are embedded several round flat seeds. Though containing strychnine and other toxins, the fruits are a favourite of the Great Bowerbird. The leaves, fruits and bark are used by Aboriginal people as a fish poison.

Vitex glabrata

One of two Vitex tree species in the Top End, this species is a spreading tree usually 7 to 12 m high. The finely fissured bark is pale grey or brown and blotchy. Being deciduous the tree survives the dry by dropping its trifoliate leaves. *V. glabrata* has mostly rounded leaflets of variable size between 5 and 15 cm long. This species may be confused with *Vitex acuminata* that has elliptic leaflets with elongated pointed tips. Flowers are pale cream to mauve, somewhat orchid-like. Smooth, fleshy berries, to 1.5 cm, form on branching stalks, becoming black when ripe. The grape-like fruits of this species are highly sought after by Aboriginal people. They can be eaten raw, cooked or sun-dried and stored. Found in monsoon vine forests on a variety of rocky habitats and extending to vine forest in coastal areas.

Animals of the Monsoon Forests

Birds

About 15 species of birds choose the monsoon forest as primary habitat, although many of the birds that are found in riparian forests are also found in monsoon forests. Biogeographically, many of the birds found in Australian monsoon forests are related to birds found in the rainforests of New Guinea. Not surprisingly, most of the species are confined in their Australian distribution to the north, for example the Green-backed Gerygone and the Rainbow Pitta. The Rose-crowned Fruit-dove and the Emerald Dove are two that range widely throughout eastern Australia.

During the wet season, monsoon forests receive predominantly breeding migrants from New Guinea, Indonesia and Asia. Examples are the Torresian Imperial Pigeon, Channel-billed Cuckoo and Common Koel, all frugivores, and the Dollarbird, which feeds on large insects. All breed here during the wet season. Of the 18 species of honeyeater, the Rufous-banded Honeyeater and the Bar-breasted Honeyeater are generally confined to wetter, non-eucalypt forests, particularly the riparian and monsoon forests, but also the mangrove habitat.

Rainbow Pitta

The only bird that is confined to the Top End's jungles, or monsoon pockets, is the Rainbow Pitta. This jewel-like bird is endemic to north and north-western Australia, replacing its close relative, the east coast Noisy Pitta. The Rainbow Pitta is sedentary and single birds or pairs occupy the same patch of jungle year in, year out. They hop along on the forest floor, poking with their bills here and there in search of land snails, worms and ground living insects, which are their staple diet. Normally quiet, during their breeding season, just before the monsoon, the male will climb trees to chirp his clear two-note whistle, "want-a-whip" in order to attract a mate and to warn off other pairs.

Brown Goshawk *Accipiter fasciatus*

A barred, brown hawk, about 50 cm, with a long, rounded tail, and short, rounded wings. Generally keeps under cover rather than soaring or perching in exposed situations. A skulking predator, it hunts by stealth, working secretively from tree to tree. It preys on birds, mammals, reptiles, frogs and large insects. Established pairs are sedentary, and the bird is fairly abundant in forests and along tree-lined watercourses. Its call is a high-pitched, rapid-fire whistle 'kikikik'. The female has a slower, mellow 'yuik yuik yuik'.

Orange-footed Scrubfowl *Megapodius reinwardt*

A large, about 45 cm, dark, small-headed fowl with a prominent crest and powerful orange legs and feet. The smallest of the Australian mound-builders, it builds the largest mound, raking in litter and soil to form a mound up to seven metres in diameter. In this it lays and buries its eggs; the heat in the interior of the mound incubates the eggs. By day, pairs of birds either maintain the mound or scratch in the litter for fruits, seeds, shoots and invertebrates. At night the birds call from their roosts such as a bough high over a creek. The voice is a raucous loud double crow, also cluckings.

Rose-crowned Fruit Dove *Ptilinopus regina*

A small, 20 cm, colourful pigeon with a rose-pink crown, yellow abdomen and yellow tip to the tail. Juveniles green with mottled yellow abdomen. Often not noticed because its colours blend into the vegetation, this Fruit Dove is common enough in monsoon forests, deciduous vine thickets and also in mangroves and paperbark forests, where fruit is ripening. Usually in pairs or in groups of five or six, the birds are tree-dwellers. They are thought to be nomadic, following the ripening fruit. The voice is a surprisingly loud repeated 'woo-hoo' becoming faster and ending in rapid 'hoo-hoo-hoo'.

Torresian Imperial Pigeon *Ducula bicolor*

A large, mostly white pigeon, 38-44 cm, with slate grey flight feathers and dark tip of tail. This handsome bird has a conspicuous swooping flight and males particularly are often seen flying steeply up, stalling and gliding downwards. The Imperial Pigeon is a migrant to northern and eastern Australia from New Guinea. Preferring coastal areas, they typically breed on offshore islands where they gather in large colonies. Their diet consists only of fruit, almost exclusively from rainforest trees and palms. They swallow the fruit whole, the pulp being quickly digested. In and around Darwin, the Imperial Pigeon is particularly fond of the juicy red fruits of the Carpentaria Palm *Carpentaria acuminata*, a Northern Territory endemic, which grows in suburban gardens. Its voice is an evocative deep cooing 'up-ooo' and deep 'oooms' and resonating 'roo-ca-hoo'.

Emerald Dove *Chalcophaps indica*

A plump dove, 25 cm, with iridescent green wings, red bill, reddish-brown head and body, tinged with purple. There is a distinct white patch on the shoulder and two white bars on the back. These ground-dwelling birds eat seeds and fallen fruit. Mostly solitary, they can be seen walking on tracks or flying across open areas with a strong, swift and heavy flight, beating their wings continuously and flying low to the ground. Voice is a low pitched but penetrating coo.

Channel-billed Cuckoo *Scythrops novaehollandiae*

The largest cuckoo in the world it is a very large, 60 cm, bird with a huge pale grey bill, plumage grey above with a long, barred tail. White below. A migratory cuckoo arriving from Indonesia and New Gunea in northern Australia in August-October. It parasitises the nests of many species including the Magpie Lark and Torresian Crow. It prefers figs but will eat a variety of fruit, eggs, young birds and insects. May gather into small foraging flocks, otherwise in territorial pairs. Voice a bubbling trumpet.

Koel
Eudynamy scolopacea

A long tailed cuckoo, 39-40 cm, the male glossy blue-black with a red eye, and the female dark brown with spots and bars. It is a migrant that arrives in Darwin from New Guinea and the Lesser Sunda Islands to breed in August-September and departs April-May. Shy and elusive, Koels feed on fruit, particularly native figs and berries, occasionally raiding cultivated fruit. Koels frequent rainforest, tall open forest and riverine areas and are seen singly, in pairs or in small displaying groups. They typically parasitize the cup-shaped nests of friar birds, orioles and magpie larks. Its monotonous shrieking call, rising slowly in tone to a frantic, almost lunatic climax, may continue throughout the day and into the night, a poignant hallmark of the impending wet season.

Azure Kingfisher
Alcedo azurea

A short-tailed kingfisher, 18 cm, with an orange breast, upperparts violet blue, legs bright orange. Mostly alone, the Azure spends most of its day staring down from its perch on a low, bare branch, not much more than a metre from water. Its prey includes fish, insects or crustaceans on which it dives in a flash of blue. Its voice is a shrill 'peee peeee' usually given in flight.

White-bellied Cuckoo-shrike *Coracina papuensis*

A pale grey cuckoo-shrike, 28 cm, with black between eye and beak, and white breast. Gathering in family groups of 2 to 5, the White-bellied feeds on insects and fruits in both the canopy and shrubbery. Birds fly through the forest midstrata. Flight is undulating with brief bursts of flapping. Birds settle with a characteristic shuffle of the wings. The voice is a shrill 'kseak', also churring noises.

TC

Varied Triller *Lalage leucomela*

A grey and white bird, about 19 cm. Male has white eyebrow, upperparts black with white marking through wing. Underparts white. Female like the male but browner above and underparts darker with barring. Light cinnamon rump. In pairs or at most small family groups, Varied Trillers feed on fruit and insects on rainforest edges and along creeks. It forages in the canopy or lower down when in more open forest making characteristic churring contact calls as it forages. A common bird in Darwin in more vegetated areas, it is more often heard than seen with a piercing 'drreea, drrreea'.

Shining Flycatcher - male at nest   Shining Flycatcher - female at nest

Shining Flycatcher *Myiagra alecto*

Male a shining blue-black flycatcher, 17 cm, female, with upperparts rich rufous chestnut, underparts white, crown only is black. Sedentary birds, which forage alone or in pairs in vine forests or mangroves. In vine-forests they sally out from perch to perch, picking up insects on the wing and from leaves and trunks. In mangroves the bird drops down close to the mud, darting onto prey. Voice is varied, from pretty whistlings to peculiar croakings.

Northern Fantail *Rhipidura rufiventris*

A rather inactive, grey fantail, 17 cm, with dark shafts to its tail feathers. Usually observed perching prominently, but quietly, in the upperstrata of monsoon forests, riverine forests and mangroves. It hawks out repeatedly for insects from the same perch. Mainly sedentary, it sometimes join mixed feeding flocks. It calls insistently from perches. Voice a beautiful tinkling song.

Green-backed Warbler *Gerygone chloronota*

Small, 10 cm, green-backed warbler, grey below, with a red eye. Common but inconspicuous little bird that inhabits vine thickets and mangroves. Mostly solitary, it feeds vigorously, gleaning insects in the upper and middle canopy, rarely going close to the ground. Builds a dome-like nest of interwoven fibre, bound with cobweb from which a funnel-like entrance emerges. Voice a falling, silvery thread of sound.

Helmeted Friarbird *Philemon buceroides*

A large, 35 cm, honeyeater with dark naked skin on head, and a backward-sloping knob on top of the bill. Head and throat greyish-brown, upperparts brown, underparts a lighter brown. A bird of the rainforest edge, feeding on the upper strata of trees on insects, spiders, fruit and nectar, and aggressively chasing any poachers. Usually solitary, it can congregate in groups of 10-30, cackling and squabbling noisily. In the morning and evening it announces its roosting positions with a mournful double note cry like 'poor devil'. Otherwise voice is harsh metallic whistles or cackles.

Rufous-banded Honeyeater *Conopophila albogularis*

Small, 12 cm, brown honeyeater with short bill, rufous breastband and yellow edges to wing-feathers. One of the most common small birds in Darwin, this little honeyeater forages actively for insects and nectar all day long in monsoon vine thickets, mangroves and paperbark forests. Semi-nomadic, small groups dash, hop and flutter in midstrata, twittering constantly and occasionally giving short bursts of song, breaking off to chase one another. Mixes with other species in blossoming trees. Voice, cheeps, and twittering 'sweeta-swee' or 'swee-whit-chee-tee'.

White-gaped Honeyeater *Lichenostomus unicolor*

A very plain honeyeater, 20 cm, with a prominent white gape. Noisy and aggressive, the White-gaped occupies thickets. It is sedentary and occurs in small groups feeding under shrubbery and within the canopy, hopping actively, gleaning insects and picking fruit. It occasionally joins other honeyeaters to rifle nectar. Flight from shrub to shrub is low and more erratic than other honeyeaters. Voice various loud rollicking calls 'whit, whit, awhit-whit', explosive 'chop'.

Bar-breasted Honeyeater *Ramsayornis fasciatus*

Small, 12 cm, honeyeater with boldly barred breast, streaked flanks, white face with a black moustache. Rather solitary along gallery forest and monsoon forest, wandering nomadically in search of blossom. Works quietly at all levels of the forest. Voice, one note, soft 'mew', also shrill piping.

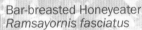

Dusky Honeyeater *Myzomela obscura*

Plainest honeyeater, 14 cm, uniformly dusky brown with darker chin. Only locally nomadic, the Dusky occurs singly or in small groups, feeding vigorously on insects and nectar. Voice an obscure squeak, excited 'see see see'.

JB

117

Yellow Oriole *Oriolus flavocinctus*

A slender, yellow green bird, 30 cm, with pale yellow edging to black wing feathers, yellow tip to green tail. Sedentary, Yellow Orioles are birds of the vine forests and gallery forests. Feeds alone or in pairs on fruit in the middle and upper strata, working slowly and methodically. The male sings sporadically throughout the day year round, its voice a rich, deep bubbling 'yok yok yuddle'.

Yellow Figbird *Sphecotheres viridis*

A sociable, stocky bird, about 29 cm, with a stout bill, red skin around the eye. Back olive-green, brilliant yellow below. Female, upperparts brownish, underparts lighter and heavily streaked. A bird of the monsoon forest, it is common in Darwin, living in small groups which are locally nomadic; after fruits such as figs, pawpaw, native cherries and bananas. They feed in the upper strata, concentrating on a single tree until it is stripped of fruit. They are noisy birds with calls of a gay, pleasant and squeaky quality. Also loud clear, slightly descending 'see-kew, see-kew'.

Spangled Drongo *Dicrurus bracteatus*

Totally black, fish-tailed bird, about 30 cm, with iridescent blue spangles on its breast. A sedentary bird of the monsoon forests of northern Australia, it sallies forth in graceful aerial manoeuvres from a prominent perch in mid-forest strata usually after hard-cased insects. Works singly or in pairs. Voice is unmistakable, like a well-strained wire fence being strained, metallic, tearing 'shshashash'.

Great Bowerbird *Chlamydera nuchalis*

Grey with brownish-grey back, about 37 cm, wings and tail heavily spotted pale grey. Stout bill and a lilac nape crest. Tropical bowerbird, usually solitary and usually a fruit-eater, bounding within the crowns of bushy trees and shrubs. Male builds a bower, of open or over-arched avenue of twigs on the ground in which he displays and mates with females (if he is lucky), who then leave to nest and rear the young on their own. Voice, grating hissings, mechanical sounds and mimicry.

Great Bowerbird, male at his bower

Reptiles & Amphibians

The lack of a rich, distinctive monsoon rainforest fauna is reflected in reptiles and amphibians. The number of reptiles and amphibians using monsoon forests in the Top End is 61 lizards, 18 snakes and 27 frogs. While this represents 64%, 42% and 77% respectively of the total regional fauna, very few reptiles and amphibians seem totally dependent on Top End jungles. Only two skinks *Carlia macfarlani* and *Sphenomorphus nigricaudis* and one frog species, a species of *Rana,* have been recorded only from monsoon forests in eastern Arnhem Land and Melville and Bathurst Islands.

Many of the reptiles and amphibians listed for the woodlands and wetlands may be found in the Monsoon Forests. Frogs and snakes are well represented and relatively common in monsoon pockets. Dragons, geckoes and some skinks are poorly represented.

A Keelback snake has caught its prey, a Rocket Frog

Mammals of the Monsoon Forests

In the wet/dry tropics of northern and north-western Australia, small scattered patches of monsoon rainforests occur in an expanse of Eucalyptus-dominated open forest and woodland. The shallow seas of the Gulf of Carpentaria and its arid hinterland severed these Northern Territory jungles from the larger rainforests of the wet tropics. These have been large enough to provide refuge to specialist mammals that have persisted since the rainforests of Australia were connected to those of New Guinea. In contrast, the ravages of climate have shredded the jungles of the Top End and Kimberley into tatters. These scraps have lost their specialised mammalian rainforest fauna.

The lack of specialised rainforest mammals, however, belie the great importance of jungles to mammals which use them in a very dynamic way. For instance, mammal species, such as rock rats and fruit bats that feed from fleshy fruits or from the seeds of woody plants are commonly found in monsoon forests.

Dusky Rat *Rattus colletti*

Black Wallaroo *Macropus bernardus*

Perhaps because there are no specialised mammals, many other mammals use the monsoon forests for a variety of reasons. The Dusky Rat (see description in Wetlands Chapter) retreat to fringing monsoon forests when the floodplains became inundated in the late wet season. The Agile Wallaby (see description in Woodland Chapter) and the Black Wallaroo of Arnhem Land rest in monsoon pockets during the day and forage in the surrounding grasslands. Other mammals may flee to the protective greenery during fire, which does not cross the boundaries into the wetter, less flammable jungles.

Little Red Flying Fox
Pteropus scapulatus

Black Flying Fox with baby
Pteropus alecto

Black-footed Tree-Rat *Mesembriomys gouldii*

Northern Blossom Bat
Macroglossus minimus nanus

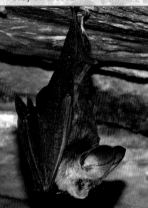

Dusky Horseshoe Bat
Hipposideros ater

Grassland Melomys *Melomys burtoni*

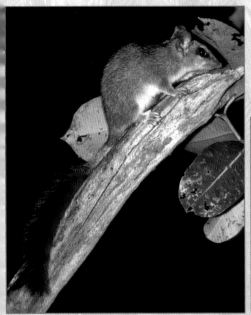

While no mammals live entirely within monsoon forests, a significant proportion of the mammal fauna favour monsoon forests. These include rodents and bats such as the Northern Blossom Bat, Dusky Leaf-nosed Bat, Black Flying Fox and Little Red Flying Fox, Grassland Melomys , Carpentarian Rock Rat and other rock rats. Most of these are described in the Woodlands Chapter. Echidnas also favour rocky monsoon forests.

Brush-tailed Phascogale *Phascogale pirata*

Golden Bandicoot *Isoodon auratus*

Northern Long-eared Bat *Nyctophilus arnhemensis*

Short-eared Rock Wallaby *Petrogale brachyotis*

There are also significant ecological associations between some mammals and some plants. Several fruit-eating birds and two bats, the Black Flying Fox and Little Red Flying Fox, are important vectors for the dispersal of fruits and seeds of monsoon rainforest plants. Both of these species and the Northern Blossom Bat also pollinate many of the woody plant species of this habitat. These roles may be critical for the development of floristic richness within expanding, recovering or new monsoon rainforest patches.

Short-beaked Echidna *Tachyglossus aculeatus*

Fawn Antechinus *Antechinus bellus*

Common Planigale *Planigale maculata*

CHAPTER SEVEN

Freshwater Wetlands

The extensive freshwater wetlands of the Top End have made the region world famous. Vast floodplains fringe most of the sinuous rivers that drain the subcoastal plain. Scattered across the Top End, no other habitat undergoes such marked seasonal changes, from verdant, lily-sprinkled waters in the wet season, to brown, desiccated grasslands and sedgelands on the deeply cracked clays in the dry.

Plants of the Freshwater Wetlands

Within the floodplain habitat are a number of distinct plant communities uniquely adapted to the dramatic seasonal changes in water regime. While there is considerable overlap in species, depressions in the floodplain, holding water well into the dry season, typically have aquatic and semi-aquatic species, in contrast to the floodplains themselves, which are dominated by semi-aquatic grasses and sedges. Both communities are necessarily adapted to seasonal flooding and droughts.

Common aquatic plant species include

Kankong *Ipomoea aquatica*

A floating vine common on most billabongs and freshwater wetland areas in the Darwin region and Kakadu. In aquatic situations, the rather hollow stems spread across the surface of the water for up to several metres, with roots arising from nodes which hang suspended in the water column. The leaves are alternate and held on a long stalk. They are generally arrow-shaped and taper to a long pointed tip and have a pale undersurface. Flowers are large and trumpet-shaped (morning glory style), pink to white in colour with a darker throat, with very delicate thin-walled petals. Fruits are papery capsules about 1.3 cm in diameter and contain 4 seeds. Although usually associated with seasonal water, this species is also a trailing vine on stream banks and on floodplains and grassland habitats. The common name, Kankong, is Chinese. A green-stemmed variety of this species is widely cultivated in Asia as a food plant where the young stems are boiled or fried in sauce. The local wild species has more of a red stem. Bunches of Kankong are readily available in Darwin's open air cosmopolitan markets.

Ludwigia adscendens

A common perennial aquatic herb found from India to China and Northern Australia, and an important component of floating mat vegetation. One of several *Ludwigia* species found on floodplains in the Darwin region, most others are widely distributed annuals or pantropic weeds. The leaves are smooth, oval with a rounded tip, to 8 cm long, with distinct venation. Thriving during the late wet season, floating stems spread out across the water. Numerous adventitious roots spread out from each node so the plant takes its root system with it as it grows. White, oval-shaped roots, composed of spongy, air-filled tissue function like small floats enabling the plant to remain on the surface of the water. Flowers and fruit may be produced at any time of year, depending on moisture availability. White to pale yellow flowers to 3 cm across form in the leaf axils.

Fruit capsules are brown, cylindrical and split open to release the 2 mm long seeds.

Monochoria australasica

An aquatic herb with smooth, shiny dark green leaves and a relatively upright growth habit. Growing from a creeping rootstock the elongated, pointed leaves are held on separate stems. Most noticeable when in full bloom during January to May when the dense clusters of bright blue-purple flowers make a brilliant display. Two to twelve individual flowers, to 2.5 cm diameter, each with a central cluster of yellow stamens are held on each spike, above the foliage. Fruits are small papery capsules. Common on small billabongs and seasonal swamps in water to 1 m deep.

JB

Lotus Lily or Red Lily
Nelumbo nucifera

A perennial aquatic herb with large smooth rounded leaves 30 to 75 cm in diameter in deeper permanent swamps. Grows from submerged rootstock with the majority of the huge, cupped leaves and flowers held above the water on erect prickly stems. The plant is famous for its large, 15 to 25 cm across, deep pink, fragrant flowers seen during March to November. From the yellow centre of the old flower, a round woody receptacle develops. Enclosed within the snug cavities of this receptacle, the seed is held within a hard, nut-like fruit. This hardy coating may contribute to the seeds having incredible longevity, with germination recorded after several hundred years of dormancy. Aboriginal uses for the plant include eating the seeds and root tubers. Overseas this species is widely used for food and medicinal purposes.

Water Lily *Nymphaea violacea*

A common perennial aquatic herb found in water to 2 m deep in Northern Australia and Papua New Guinea. The floating leaves are rounded, glossy green above, deeply two-lobed at the base and 10 to 30 cm across. The margins may be slightly wavy and the venation is very prominent beneath. The leaves are attached to the buried rhizome via long fleshy stalks. Peak flowering occurs during January to July when the showy lilies appear on long solitary stalks. Individual flowers have numerous petals and are held either at water level or slightly above it. The yellow centres contain numerous fragile stamens and have a delightful fragrance. Flower colour may vary from white to pink or blue-mauve, even changing during the course of a day. A lily-covered billabong may change from mauve hues in the morning to pale white tones by late afternoon. Bush bread is made by Aboriginal people from the ground up seeds.

Fringe Lily or White Snowflake Lily
Nymphoides indica

An aquatic herb with long slender stems and floating leaves, growing from a submerged rootstock. Leaves are smooth and roundish, thick textured and with 2 deep lobes at the base. The flowers are small, to 2.5 cm across, and white with a yellow throat and delicate fringed edges. Fruits are small oval capsules less than 1 cm long. *Nymphoides indica*, like several other local water lilies, commonly reproduces vegetatively, with new stems and roots budding off from the undersurface of the old leaf. This species is common in the shallow waters of paperbark swamps and occurs in the swampy patches fringing freshwater streams and in billabongs. Another fringe lily, *Nymphoides aurantiaca*, with vivid yellow flowers, is also common in the same habitats, producing spectacular carpets of yellow flowers.

Nymphoides aurantiaca

Common plant species of the Floodplain include

Lily, Onion Lily *Crinum angustifolium*

A large, distinctive lily to 1 m high arising from perennial bulbs at the beginning of the wet season. The leaves are smooth, leathery and strap-like, 45 to 100 cm long and taper to a pointed tip, emerging from the ground soon after the first rains. The flower spike appears shortly after. It consists of 6 to 14 large spectacular white flowers with long maroon stamens, borne on a tall erect stalk. By blooming at night it allows insect and moths to pollinate the flowers, borne on a tall erect stalk. The prominent white flowers stand out in stark contrast to the vivid greenery of the coastal floodplains in the wet season. A preparation from the crushed bulbs is used as an antiseptic for wounds and sores.

Spike-rush *Eleocharis dulcis*

Eleocharis is a genus of herbs belonging to the Cyperaceae family, or 'sedges'. *Eleocharis* species may be annual or perennial, and their leaves bladeless sheaths or spikes. The multi-flowered inflorescences or spikelets appear at the end of these "leaves". Up to five species of *Eleocharis* occur on the clayey soils of the floodplains in the Darwin region. The peanut-sized bulbs at the base of *E. dulcis*, a semi-aquatic sedge found in or around depressions in the floodplain, are an important food source for magpie geese. Aboriginal people use the plant by grinding the nuts into a flour for bush bread.

Australian Wild Rice *Oryza rufipogon*

An annual grass with smooth slender erect stems to 1.5 m high, and creeping rhizomes. The hairless leaf blades are up to 65 cm long and 1.7 cm wide. The inflorescence is a compact panicle or cluster of fine branches on which the 'grains' develop. Growing only on swampy ground usually on black soil plains.

Pandanus and Paperbark

The upland margin of the freshwater floodplain habitat is often delineated by a dense fringe of Pandanus or paperbarks.

Pandanus

Pandanus spiralis

Evocatively outlined against the evening sky, *Pandanus spiralis*, or Screw Palm, is a quintessential image of the Top End. A distinctive tree to 10 m high with stiff, thick leathery leaves that are V-shaped in cross-section and tapering to an elongated tip. These characteristically grow in a spiral - hence 'screw' palm. Unburnt leaves may form a dense grass skirt. The young leaves are stiffly erect and crowded around the growing tip. Older leaves become folded, forming the dense messy head of foliage that gives the plant its famous profile.

Pandanus aquaticus

Two other species of *Pandanus* occur in the Top End *Pandanus aquaticus* which, as the name suggests, is restricted to stream banks and billabongs, and *Pandanus basedowii*, found only in the sandstone escarpment region of western Arnhem Land and Kakadu. *Pandanus spiralis* has male and female flowers on separate plants, and wedge shaped fruits clustered together in a pineapple-shaped bunch, which becomes bright red and fruity-smelling when ripe. Found almost everywhere, it often indicates swampy ground, particularly where it forms dense monospecific stands on the margins of floodplain and wetland areas. Aboriginal people eat the fruit kernels raw, or they may be roasted to taste. Minor ailments were treated with preparations from the core of the stem and the leaves are an important source of fibre for dilly bags, mats, baskets, rope and armbands. The buoyant trunks were also used to make rafts.

Pandanus aquaticus fruit

Pandanus spiralis fruit

127

Paperbarks

Paperbark forests are characteristic of freshwater wetland areas, and are dominated by trees of the genus Melaleuca. These trees survive from three to six months of waterlogging annually, and may form pure, monospecific stands. Paperbarks are named for their distinctive soft, papery bark, which can be removed from the tree in thick layers. Paperbarks are of particular importance birds. It is primary habitat for about 20 species of birds and fully one half the total avifauna for the Top End uses the habitat. Aboriginal people have a multitude of uses for the bark including storing, wrapping and cooking food, roofing for shelters, fire tinder, bedding and for wrapping corpses for burial.

Silver-leafed paperbark *Melaleuca argentea*

A large spreading tree 10 to 20 m high, with distinctive silvery foliage (argentea means silver). A common species on the larger, sandy watercourses, it often has a multi-stemmed trunk and twisted spreading boughs. The leaves are pendulous and narrowly elliptic, widest in the middle and tapering to both ends. Young leaves are silky hairy, becoming smooth. A spectacular flush of new silvery leaves typically occurs during the early

dry season. From June to October the prolific cream bottle-brush type flowers, 5 to 12 cm, produce a heady smell and a rich source of nectar. The woody fruits are small cup-shaped capsules attached directly to the stem. Typically occurs in association with *Melaleuca leucadendra*. Aboringal people use the leaves to flavour roasting meat.

Cajuput Tree *Melaleuca cajuputi*

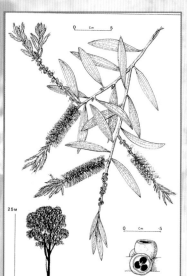

A tree 10 to 30 m high with a stout central trunk and a dense canopy of small leaves. The white-grey bark is papery, fibrous and layered. The young leaves of *Melaleuca cajuputi* are softly hairy but older leaves are smooth. Flowers are green to cream, and produced in cylindrical spikes 4 to 8 cm long. Fruit are stalkless woody cups closely clustered along the stem. This is a common tree on heavy clay soils of the coastal plains in the Darwin region, in the Top End, preferring sites that remain moist throughout the year. This tree is the source of 'cajuput oil' used commercially for medicinal purposes.

White Paperbark
Melaleuca leucadendra

Among the tallest and best formed tree species in the Top End, *Melaleuca leucadendra* can grow to 30 m. The bark is layered and white to grey. Individual leaves are alternate, mostly straight, and widest just near the base. The tree has a weeping habit due to the uniformly pendulous leaves and branchlets. Flowers are produced during the dry season, and are a greenish-cream with numerous stamens in spikes 7 to 16 cm long. The woody seed capsules contain numerous very fine seeds and may remain on the tree for a considerable period. *Melaleuca leucadendra* prefers sites with a high water table, and is generally occurring on wetter sites than *Melaleuca viridiflora*.

Broadleaved Paperbark *Melaleuca viridiflora*

A small, rather untidy tree, 2-10 m tall, occasionally to 15 metres, distinguished by its thick, broad leaves and tough, white papery bark. The leaves are widest mid-way along their length, 7 to 19 cm long, and are held stiffly in all directions along stout branchlets. The young leaves may be hairy and there are 5 to 7 prominent longitudinal veins.

Flowers have long stamens and are grouped in cylindrical spikes 5 to 10 cm long, developing into shallow woody cups containing numerous fine seeds. This species is commonly confused with *Melaleuca leucadendra* (described above).

Paperbark Orchid *Dendrobium canaliculatum*

A delicate epiphytic orchid mostly found on the trunks of *Melaleuca leucadendra* and *Melaleuca viridiflora*. The short, thick pseudobulbs grow to 12 cm long and the narrow elongated leaves arising from the bulbs have a deep groove along the upper surface. Flowering occurs during June to October when long flower stalks appear from the apex of the bulbs. The flowers are green to white, have twisted petals and purple centres or labellums. Fruit is a capsule that releases seeds in fine dusty mixture to be dispersed by the breeze.

Birds of the Freshwater Wetlands

Sixty-eight species of birds, more than a quarter of all Top End birds, occupy inundated floodplains as a primary habitat. Almost all of these species, however, are widespread throughout Australia or Asia. Few are endemic. Dominant species are the Magpie Geese, Whistling Ducks, Intermediate Egrets and Pied Herons, but there are many other species, which are extremely numerous.

The contribution that birds of the inundated floodplains make to the Top End's avifauna is inflated by migratory waders, which arrive in the late dry season. The most common species in freshwater wetlands of the Top End are godwits, sand plovers and knots. Sharp-tailed Sandpipers, Curlew Sandpipers and Red-necked Stints also occur in numbers, staging here before moving south.

The grasses and sedges of the drying floodplains are occupied by a substantial number of birds, some of them resident and others migrants in the dry season. Where vegetation is dense, small passerines like the Golden-headed Cisticola and the Chestnut-breasted Mannikin may be resident. In rank grasses, quail will be found, commonly the Brown Quail.

While all dryland habitats in the Top End contain a considerable number of birds of prey, large numbers are particularly noticed in the sedgelands and grasslands. These include hawks, falcons, eagles, harriers and owls.

Jabiru fishing for tucker

Great Egret and Little Egret

Royal Spoonbills at Fogg Dam

Birds of the Wetlands species include

Little Pied Cormorant *Phalacrocorax melanoleucos*

Pied waterbird, 55 cm, with long tail, short legs and with all four toes joined by web. Yellow bill, blunt and hooked. Swims low in the water, dives for fish and crustaceans, favouring the latter. Hangs wings out to dry. Common to the east of Darwin. Voice croaking 'tuk tuk tuk' cooing at nest.

Little Black Cormorant *Phalacrocorax sulcirostris*

Black cormorant with a black face, 65 cm. Longer and thinner bill than Little Pied, indicating that a wider range of prey is taken. Cooperative rafts of birds will gather to herd shoals of fish. Voice guttural croaking, whistling and ticking.

Darter *Anhinga melanogaster*

A large, about 90 cm, black or greyish-brown waterbird with long, snake-like neck, long tail and short legs with all four toes joined by a web. Pale streaks on the wing. Female lighter than male with pale underparts. It swims low in the water and dives for its prey, spearing fish and turtles with its sharp bill. Found in smooth, fresh or salty riverine waters. Characteristically hangs its wings out to dry. After a leaping take off, flies well. Seen more than cormorants to which they are closely related, differing by the snake-like neck. Males and females have different plumage. Voice is a clicking rattle.

White-faced Heron *Ardea novaehollandiae*

Herons are long-necked, long-legged waterbirds with coloured plumage. The White-faced Heron is grey with a white face, one of the commonest herons, 70 cm. Usually one or a pair stalk in shallow waters or in pastures, generally spaced out from other members of this species. A generalist feeder, will stir one foot in the water to stir prey of fish, crustaceans, amphibians etc. Voice a loud croak, guttural notes.

Pied Heron *Ardea picata*

A small, 48 cm, black and white heron with a black crown with plumes, yellow bill, neat looking. Exclusively tropical and abundant in northern Australia. Commonly gather in loose feeding groups of around 5-30. Food includes crustaceans and fish but insects and their larvae are favoured, hence the bird can be found in swamps but also in sewage ponds and garbage tips and around buffalo, cattle and horses. Voice harsh croaks.

Great Egret *Ardea alba*

Egrets are mostly white birds. Can be distinguished from one another by size, stance and extent of gape below eye. During breeding season, differences are more obvious. The Great is a large white egret, 90 cm, with gape of yellow bill extending behind the eye and with black legs. Long neck is shaped into a 'question mark' position. Solitary and territorial, hunts in water up to 30 cm deep - deeper than other herons. Wait and watch strategy. Voice low pitched croak in alarm.

Intermediate Egret *Ardea intermedia*

White intermediate-sized egret, 65 cm, with thicker orange-yellow bill not extending behind eye, dark legs. Stands with neck straight. Frequents shallow waters, mudbanks and pastures, alone or in dispersed groups. Feeds on fish mainly. Voice loud croaking.

Little Egret *Ardea garzetta*

Small white egret, 55 cm, with black legs and black bill, yellow face. Usually forages alone on mudflats, rarely in water more than 10 cm deep. Preys on fish, amphibians, invertebrates. Voice, usually quiet.

Brolga *Grus rubicundus*

A pale grey, long-legged crane, 125 cm, with a bustle of secondary feathers falling over the rump. Scarlet on rear of head and nape. Known for their elaborate dances which they do in and outside of breeding season. Family groups of Brolgas, led and protected by the dominant male, often join others in flocks of up to several hundred. Wander widely for food. Flight is graceful on steadily up-flicking wings and outstretched neck and legs. Voice whooping trumpet in flight and on the ground. May be confused with Sarus Crane *Grus antigone* which is much less common, and has more red on the neck.

Jabiru *Ephippiorhynchus asiaticus*

Also known as the Black-necked Stork, this is an unmistakable bird, large, 110 cm, black and white stork with iridescent black neck. Male has brown eye, female has yellow eye. Usually solitary, the bird is a freshwater forager preying on fish, will also eat reptiles, frogs, crabs, carrion. Mostly stand and wait or stalk slowly. Voice, dull booms, also clappers its bill.

Comb-crested Jacana, *Irediparra gallinacea*

These small birds have very large toes that enable them to walk on lily pads. They nest during rainy/monsoon times on a damp pile of floating plants. They tuck their babies under their wings and carry them. When they fly their legs and toes trail. They have a distinctive red comb and forehead, long dull green legs. Squeeky 'pee pee pee' shrill alarm call.

Royal Spoonbill *Platalea regia*

Spoonbill with black bill, black legs and black skin to behind eyes. Yellow patch above each eye. White erectile nuchal plumes. Feeds in shallows of fresh and saltwater wetlands and intertidal flats by sweeping submerged bill from side to side.

Glossy Ibis *Plegadis falcinellus*

Ibis have downcurved bills. The Glossy Ibis is a small, to 60 cm, all-dark ibis with reddish-brown neck and dark iridescent body. They feed in groups, 2-30 or so, in shallow freshwater swamps and mud flats, particularly during the early dry season, where trees and bushes provide shelter. Probe with their bills for frogs, snails, spiders and insects. Voice a long harsh crow-like croak, also grunts.

Sacred Ibis or Australian White Ibis *Threskiornis molucca*

White ibis with black naked head and neck, 75 cm, and with black plumes and feathers near tail. Flies in numbers in a V-shape formation. Forages only in swampy or water-covered ground, moving head from side-to-side searching for crustaceans, fish, snails, frogs. Present throughout the year around Darwin. Voice harsh barks and shouts.

Straw-necked Ibis *Threskiornis spinicollis*

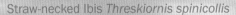

Pied ibis with long yellow plumes on neck, 75 cm. The most abundant and widespread ibis, common on ovals, lawns and cultivated grass particularly during the dry season. Eats not only aquatic items but also grasshoppers and insects. Feeds in small flocks. Voice long grunting 'u-u-urh' in flight.

Magpie Goose *Anseranas semipalmata*

Large pied goose-like bird, to 90 cm, of the tropical wetlands. Characterised by semi-webbed feet and large knob on the head and loud honking. Common bird of the Top End. See pg 56-57 in Chapter Four.

Plumed Whistling-Duck *Dendrocygna eytoni*

Face and foreneck whitish-buff. Bill pink. Crown and hind neck pale brown. Wings brown above, pale below. Identified by long flank plumes that extend over back. Feed in floodplain grasslands. Roost in large groups on banks. Make a whistling call as they fly overhead.

Wandering Whistling-duck *Dendrocygna arcuata*

A grazing duck, with elongated pale flank feathers and loud whistling call. Noisy wingbeats make a whistling sound in flight. Dark crowned, bill black, upperparts brownish, feathers edged chestnut, underparts chestnut. Legs and feet black. Prefers the deepest and most permanent tropical lagoons where flocks of hundreds feed noisily. Food is mainly vegetation, mainly aquatic plants. Voice high pitched whistles.

Radjah Shelduck *Tadorna radjah*

Also known as the Burdekin Duck, large, 60 cm, striking white-headed duck with a pink bill, chestnut breast band, dark back, rump and tail. Prefer brackish water, mudbanks, mangrove fringed mouths and sometimes on lagoons. Commonly seen throughout the year except in the latter part of the wet season when the birds disperse to breed. Found in pairs to several hundreds as the dry season progresses. Feeds on the edges of water by swinging bill from side to side sieving algae and molluscs, also worms and large insects. Voice, male a loud whistle, female a harsh rattling.

Green Pygmy Goose *Nettapus pulchellus*

A small dainty duck, 35 cm, with a stubby, goose-like bill. Prominent white cheek, neck, and back glossy green, flanks grey with dark bars. A sedentary, Top End bird, it forms flocks of hundreds on the most permanent lagoons toward the end of the dry season. Usually found floating amongst waterlilies which are their main diet. Voice, male has a distinctive shrill 'pee-whit'.

JB

Pacific Black Duck *Anas superciliosa*

A dabbling duck, taking food on or just below the surface. Large, 60 cm, with two dark lines on a buff face. There is an iridescent rectangle of colour on the wing, dark green to purple. A common duck Australia-wide. Prefers deeper permanent freshwater and lagoons. Feeds on seeds, emergent plants and aquatic insects, up-ending with tail in the air and bill in the water. The female 'quacks', the male has a soft, reedy note.

Rufous Night Heron *Nycticorax caledonicus*

When breeding has black crown and bill and two white nuchal plumes. Belly white, upperparts of wings rufous. Non-breeding lacks the plumes. Feeds nocturnally; Daytime roosts in trees close to the water. Habitat; swamps, estuaries, intertidal flats, rivers, creeks or ponds

Rufous Night-Heron juvenille   Rufous Night-Heron adult

White-bellied Sea Eagle *Haliaeetus leucogaster*

A large, 80 cm, magnificent raptor with massive legs and broad wings. White head, breast and abdomen, grey above. Soars with wings upswept like a huge butterfly. An eagle of estuaries and large inland waterways, perches prominently on dead trees and soars lazily in circles. Calls between pairs are strident, far-carrying metallic clanking.

Swamp Harrier *Circus approximans*

Large, 55 cm, lightly built hawk with a white rump and faintly barred tail, brown above. Long, broad wings upswept in flight, long tails and slender, long legs. Usually seen floating low over reeds, dropping down to take insects, mammals, reptiles and birds. Partly migratory, shifting north in the dry season and moving south to breed in the wet season. Voice, loud 'kee-oo'.

Brown Quail *Coturnix ypsilophora*

A portly, 18 cm, ground bird. Chestnut to grey-brown with faint white streaks, black barring. Usually found in small parties, on the edges of grasslands in the early morning or late evening. Feeds on seeds and insects often in low-lying swampy ground. Voice, a loud whistled 'f-weep', 'bee-quick, bee-quick'. When flushed quick, flute-like chatter.

White-browed Crake Porzana cinereus

A small, 19 cm, secretive bird of the tropical reedbeds, with short bill and laterally compressed body. Dark cap, two white stripes on the face. Upperparts black with olive-brown feather margins. Abdomen white. Ventures from cover more than other crakes, often on lily pads. In small groups they dash in a stop-start manner over matted vegetation. Eat mainly leeches, worms, slugs, water spiders and vegetable matter. Voice, 'chuk', 'krek', unusual loud chattering 'cutchee cutchee'

Greenshank *Tringa nebularia*

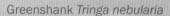

A large sandpiper with long greenish legs. Noisy, large, 35 cm, rather heavy sandpiper with long, slightly upturned bill. Long legs trail behind tail in flight. White rump and lower back prominent in flight. Mid-grey brown above, pale below. Ringing alarm call makes this bird easy to identify. Feeds in ones and twos, on crustaceans, tadpoles, frogs and small fish. Frequents fresh brackish and saline waters. Voice ringing 'tu tu tu' in alarm.

Black-tailed Godwit *Limosa limosa*

A large wader, to 45 cm, with straight or slightly down-turned bi-coloured bill. Long-legged. White rump and black tail, uniform dark grey above. Migrates from Asia and disperses usually in ones and twos. Probes deeply with its sensitive bill for crustaceans and molluscs, also spiders, tadpoles and plant matter. Often immerses its head completely in the pursuit of prey. Frequents open muddy lagoons and swamp as well as coastal estuaries and sand spits. Voice, sharp witta-witta in flying flocks, 'kip kip kip' in alarm.

Bar-tailed Godwit *Limosa lapponica*

A large wader, to 45 cm, with slightly upturned bi-coloured bill. Long-legged White rump and tail. Grey-brown above. Restricted to saline and tidal mudflats and sands. Migrate from north-east Siberia and perhaps Alaska. Many stay in north Australia where they are found in groups of 30 or so, mingling with other birds, possibly juveniles which stay each year. Feeds on molluscs and crustaceans and other marine invertebrates. Voice, sharp 'kewit' in alarm, 'kip kip kip' in excitement.

Great Knot *Calidris tenuirostris*

Stout wader, 29 cm, with bill longer than head. Grey above, pale edging to feathers, pale eyebrow, white bar on wing, shortish olive legs. Arrive from Siberia in early September. Most remain in north and north-west Australia. Feeds on tidal muds and sandflats, taking minute gastropods and invertebrates. Voice, usually silent.

Masked Lapwing *Vanellus miles*

This long-legged bird has an obvious yellow facial wattle. Brown above, white below. A common, noisy bird of natural and cultivated grasslands. In pairs and groups of 12 or so they stalk watchfully with shoulders hunched picking up insects, spiders, worms and so on. Voice is a harsh 'krekrekrekrekrekrek', often heard at night.

Chestnut-breasted Mannikin
Lonchura castaneothorax

Solid brownish finch, 10 cm, with a black face, and chestnut breast, divided from white belly by heavy black bar, grey crown, olive-brown above. Female is paler. A typical finch of the reeds on the margins of swamps, mangroves and rivers, often in flocks of several hundred. Locally nomadic, mostly eat half-ripe grass seeds. Voice is a bell-like 'teet', becoming a merry tinkling when flock launches into flight.

Dancing Brolgas, *Grus rubicundus*

A variety of bird species feeding in a freshwater channel at the end of the wet season. Fogg Dam.

137

Reptiles of the Freshwater Wetlands

Only a few species of reptile preferentially inhabit the wetlands. These include species described below.

Water Python
Liasis fuscus

One of the most beautiful of all the pythons, the Water Python shimmers with iridescent dark, blackish-brown back and yellow belly. Growing to 2 to 3 metres, it lives in and near streams, lakes, lagoons and billabongs. It is extremely abundant at Fogg Dam, where over 2000 have been tagged. It feeds on rats and other vertebrates, and is not poisonous.

DL

Water Python eating an Egret in Holmes Jungle

Slaty Grey Snake *Stegonotus cucullatus*
This non-venomous snake is often found near streams and lagoons, and sometimes in water tanks near houses. It is usually brown to leaden-grey or black, growing up to 1.3 metres overall. It is very aggressive when cornered, and bites fiercely. It is terrestrial and eats frogs.

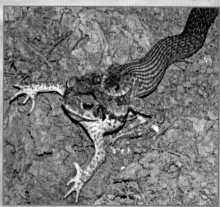

Water Python

Keelback or Freshwater Snake *Tropidonophus mairi*
This harmless snake lives in streams, swamps and lagoons, feeding on frogs. It grows to 1 metre, and may be various shades of grey, brown, olive, reddish or black, with dark skin between the scales. Keelbacks and Slaty Greys are the only known snakes to eat Cane Toads without injury.

Keelback eating a Cane Taod

Macleay's Water Snake
Enhydris polylepis

A mildly venomous, rear-fanged snake, this snake is found in creeks, swamps and rivers, often in the waterholes left after the wet season has finished. It is usually dark olive-brown to olive-black, and grows to about 80 centimetres. It will eat a variety of vertebrates.

Little File Snake
Acrochordus granulatus

File Snakes have the most extraordinarily loose and rough skin which seems to hang off the body of the snakes. They are sometimes mistaken for sea snakes but are non-poisonous and harmless. The Little File Snake lives mostly in marine and estuarine waters, hunting for small crabs and fish. It grows to about 1.2 metres.

Arafura File Snake *Acrochordus arafurae*

The Arafura File Snake is grey to dark brown with a darker reticulated pattern. It lives mostly in freshwater streams and permanent lagoons where they have easy access to estuaries and the sea. They eat fish and grow to about 1.5 to 2.5 metres, and are mostly nocturnal.

This fellow has caught these for tucker. In earlier days File Snakes formed a large part of the economic diet of Indigenous groups.

Mertens Water Monitor *Varanus mertensi*

This aquatic lizard is found in the streams, lakes and rivers of the region. Its tail is vertically compressed and paddle-like to enable it to swim well. Colour varies from rich dark brown to black above with numerous tiny light cream or yellow spots, with lower surfaces white to yellowish. It stays in or lurks over water, feeding on fish, frogs and carrion, as well as other vertebrates and insects. It grows to about 1 metre overall.

Mitchell's Water Monitor *Varanus mitchelli*

Like Merten's, this water monitor lives in or lurks over water. It differs from having a less-compressed tail which rounds towards the base, and is darker under the chin with a heavily barred throat and darker under the tail. It is also smaller, growing to 60 centimetres in total. Mitchell's Monitors eat fish, frogs and insects.

Short-necked Turtle *Emydura victoriae*

The short-necked turtle is a distinguished-looking turtle with orange stripes along its neck and through its eye. It is brown to blackish above, and grows a shell about 30 centimetres long. It has 5 claws on the fore-limbs and lives in larger rivers, lagoons and billabongs.

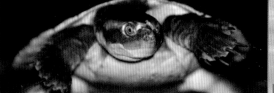

JB

Northern Snake-necked Turtle *Chelodina rugosa*

A large fresh-water turtle with a shell to 40 centimetres, the Snake-necked Turtle is found in swamps, billabongs and slow rivers. It is dark-brown to black above and has 4 claws on the forelimbs. It has the interesting habit of laying its eggs under water.

Northern Snapping Turtle *Elseya dentata*

This dark brown to black turtle has 5 claws on the forelimbs, but without the orange or pale stripes on the head. It lives in rivers, lagoons and billabongs.

Yellow-faced Turtle
Emydura tanybaraga

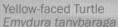

This turtle has two facial stripes: one from its eye to above the ear, and the other from the upper jaw below the ear to the side of the neck. The iris of its eye is yellow enclosing a dark horizontal streak through the eye, level with the pupil. The adult carapace is fawn to dark grey brown with scattered dark spots above, and is broadly oval with an expanded posteriorly. Hatchlings have carapaces that are broader anteriorly than posteriorly. These are known from isolated areas in NT and Cape York, QLD, but you can see them at the Territory Wildlife Park.

Frogs of the Freshwater Wetlands

More than 20 species of frogs live in the wetlands, woodlands and forests and the monsoon rainforests of the Top End. Only a few are seen regularly by the casual observer. Some are seen frequently around buildings and houses, while some may be seen in fast-flowing creeks, by lagoons and waterholes, and sometimes in trees and Pandanus. We have described those most often seen.

Green Tree Frog *Litoria caerulea*

The largest, to 110 millimetres long, and most frequently seen frog in the Top End. The Green Tree Frog as its name suggests, is uniformly green. It has broad discs on its webbed toes, and is often found around houses and in toilets. Its call is a deep bark, and the males call from the ground in the breeding season during the wet season, and from high in trees at others times. They breed in still water, and live in a wide variety of habitats.

Northern Dwarf Green Tree Frog *Litoria bicolor*

This small green frog, to 30mm, has a broad bronze stripe down its back and a green body. It lives in a variety of habitats and during the dry season rests in the axils and surfaces of Pandanus and broad-leafed plants. It has a high penetrating call, something like 'reek, reek, reek'.

Giant Frog *Cyclorana australis*

Green variety of Giant Frog *Cyclorana australis*

This burrowing frog is usually active at night in open, poorly vegetated areas from open forests to floodplains and monsoon forests. It is a robust frog, one of the largest ground-dwelling frogs in Australia, up to 100 mm long, with colours ranging from brown to grey to dull pink, sometimes with patches. The head is flat, and the tips of the fingers and toes are without the discs seen on the tree frogs.

Roth's Tree Frog *Litoria rothii*

A moderate-sized but striking frog, the top half of the iris is usually rusty red, the bottom half pale brown. The hind side of the thighs and groin have dark bars over a bright yellow ground. The body is usually putty-coloured. It grows to 55 mm. It is found in a variety of habitats, usually associated with water. Its call resembles raucous laughter.

Tornier's Frog *Litoria tornieri*

Litoria tornieri

An angular, elongated, long-toed frog with unwebbed fingers and long hind legs, this frog is coloured light fawn and has a darker brown band running from the snout through the eye to the tympanum. The hind side of the thigh has irregular yellow markings bordered by brown. It grows to about 35 mm and is found on the ground near the edge of shallow, permanent swamps and lagoons. Of similiar appearance is *Litoria pallida*, which occurs in the same habitat.

Marbled Frog *Limnodynastes convexiusculus*

This grey, brown or dark olive frog is distinguished by its marbled appearance caused by the numerous dark blotches on the raised surfaces on its back. It grows to about 55 millimetres, and has a call like a series of high-pitched, single 'plonks'. Its arched rump gave it its specific name: *convexiusculus*. It lives in savanna woodlands and lowland scrubs.

Wotjulum Frog *Litoria wotjulumensis*

Named after the Wotjulum Aboriginal settlement in Western Australia, this large frog grows to 75mm. It is rounded, with very long legs, small disks on its toes and a dark brown stripe from its snout through its eye. Its back is usually immaculate brown or fawn. The frog lives in open forests, swamps and streams, and is ground-dwelling.

Rocket Frog *Litoria nasuta*

A highly variable frog from pale brown to reddish brown, this frog has a dark stripe running from the snout through the eye to the tympanum (ear-covering). It has very long limbs and a pointy snout, and grows to about 50 mm. This frog is an extraordinary jumper, and lives in open forests as well as around swamps and lagoons.

Dahl's Frog *Litoria dahlii*

A slender frog, about 70 mm long, it is olive-brown or olive grey above with golden brown blotches. The skin is finely granular. The backs of the thighs is mottled or spotted with white. A largely aquatic frog it is usually seen around the edge of wetlands. Utters a soft call during the day as it floats.

Litoria pallida

Notaden melanoscaphus

Ornate Burrowing Frog *Platyplectrum ornatus* eating a termite

Litoria rubella

Uperoleia daviesae

Uperoleia inundata

Cyclorana longipes

Marbled Frog *Limnodynastes convexiusculus*

Crinia bilingua

Litoria inermis

Rockhole Frog *Litoria meiriana*

Monsoon Whistle-frog *Austrochaperina adelphe*

Dahl's Frog *Litoria dahlii* on Water Lily, *Nyphaea violacea*

Mammals of the Wetlands

Marrawata or Dusky Rat
Rattus colletti

The main food of the Water Python Fogg Dam, the Dusky Rat can be in the hundreds of thousands on the floodplains of the Top End. By day in the dry season it hides in the cracking soils of the floodplains, coming out at night to eat corms of the grasses of the plains. During the wet season, they retreat to higher ground. They are dark brown to black, and grow to about 132 millimetres on average.

Large-footed Myotis
Myotis adverses

One of the many micro bats, that specialises in feeding over the wetlands. It is known to catch small fish with its large hind feet while skimming over the water. This particular photo was taken in a storm water concrete pipe beneath one of Darwin's suburbs

Banded Grunters *Amniataba percoides*

Long Armed Prawn *Macrobrachium rosenbergii*

Archerfish

The Archerfish *Toxotes chatareus* is a small, pale fish with black blotches on its back. This rather unassuming fish is famous for its ability to launch watery mortar attacks on unsuspecting insects resting within the foliage above the water. It does this by collapsing its gill covers which causes a stream of water to be ejected up to two metres from its carefully aimed mouth. Also known as the Riflefish, this cunning fish patrols river edges quite close to the surface until a suitable meal flies to within spitting distance.

CHAPTER EIGHT

The Coast

Around Darwin the coast is smooth, low and flat. It is fringed by a belt of mangroves up to a few hundred metres wide and backed by bare, tidal flats that give way to freshwater swamps and plains. The main rivers, such as the Adelaide River, are tidal and are bordered by mangroves for up to 80 km inland, the border sometimes no more than one tree wide.

Mangroves

Mangroves are fascinating. For a start they are trees that thrive in salty, anaerobic conditions. Normal trees would keel over in these sorts of conditions. Not these Aussie battlers. And Australian they almost certainly are, since it seems that, since Australia is so rich in mangroves, they probably originated here. Mangroves represent a bizarre collection of unrelated plants that have evolved on the land and subsequently become adapted to an intertidal lifestyle. Mangroves have dominated one of the harshest environments known to plants. How do they do it?

The buttress roots of the Stilt-rooted Mangrove *Rhizophora stylosa*

Mangroves have many remarkable kinds of adaptations. Most mangroves have thick leaves, which are covered by a waxy cuticle or by a fuzz of hair that can interlock over the top of the pores of the leaves to reduce water evaporation. This, and the shape and architecture of the cells within the plant's leaves and stems, ensure that the leaves and stems are always turgid and don't wilt.

Salt is normally a poison to trees. Not so to mangroves. Some mangroves exclude salt via roots. This acts as a fine filter. Other mangroves take in loads of salt but pump it out via salt glands on the leaves - a close look at the leaves of *Avicennia* will usually show many fine salt crystals. Yet other mangroves store the salt in older leaves and in the bark. Some mangroves drop all their leaves seasonally and get rid of salt at the same time.

Mangroves edging Nightcliff suburbs

Like us, trees need to breathe and that is very difficult to do if you live in oxygen deficient mud. Mangroves handle this by having root systems with an amazing variety of form and function, including pneumatophores, knee-roots and plate-like buttress roots. Essentially all of these structures are roots that grow up, gasping for air, against the force of gravity. In addition, nearly all mangrove roots have lenticels or small pores, which literally "breathe". These are exposed to air some of the time.

Living in the mud *Bruguierra sp.*

Below the semi-fluid mud, all mangroves possess a system of laterally-spreading cable roots with smaller, vertically-descending anchor roots. The roots of mangroves are "heavy" compared with the rest of the plant and this, combined with aerial, stilt and buttress roots helps to stabilise the plant. Twenty six species of mangroves have been recorded from the Northern Territory. In Darwin we are lucky to be surrounded by mangroves - over 20,000 hectares in Darwin Harbour alone. Here, the intricate, drowned valley of Port Darwin provides them with shelter. Indeed, the mangrove zone may extend almost unbroken for up to several hundred metres from the central tidal channel to the base of surrounding higher land.

Rhizophora stylosa lining an estuary where crocodiles frequent

Mangrove distribution follows a distinct, predictable pattern of zonation - with species aligned in bands, roughly parallel to the shore or tidal channel. This zonation occurs throughout the harbour and in coastal situations and is due to the individual tolerances of mangrove species to salinity, frequency of tidal inundation and other associated environmental factors. The beginning of each zone even corresponds to a certain height above mean sea level and the individual zones occupy a predictable percentage of the intertidal area for each tidal creek system in Darwin Harbour.

Mangrove *Rhizophora stylosa* on the coast

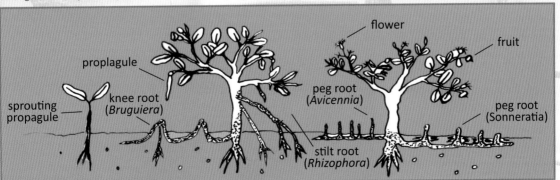

Diagram 6, Showing the form of Mangrove trees and their root types

151

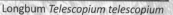

Longbum *Telescopium telescopium*   *Geloina* mollusc   Mangrove mollusc *Terebralia*

Mangroves are a rich source of traditional Aboriginal bush food. In fact scattered along the Darwin coastline are great piles of old shells, known by archaeologists as 'kitchen middens'. These are the remains of countless Aboriginal meals of shellfish, crabs and other seafood gathered from the intertidal zone, and then tossed into rubbish heaps as they were eaten. The large elongated shells of the mangrove mollusc *Terebralia* and the huge bivalved mollusc *Geloina* are common components of local middens.

Mangrove or Teredo worms

Another food source found in the mangroves are the highly specialised wood boring bivalves. Although they are known as a Mangrove or Teredo worm, they are actually an oyster, not a worm. These molluscs hollow out the trunks of mangroves, from which vantage point they filter feed, sieving their food from the water when the tide is high. Two species occur in Darwin mangroves including *Bactronophorus thoracites* and the smaller of the two species, *Bankia australis*. Aboriginal people will perform selective chipping of the host trees looking for 'the big fellow'. These molluscs also make delightful patterns in driftwood.

Mangroves are often the plant community that receives the full brunt of landfalling tropical cyclones and actually help protect the coast from devastating winds and storm surge. Most species are well adapted to storm damage and can quickly recover from defoliation by reshooting from epicormic buds along the trunk. Other species in the Rhizophoraceae family do not have this ability and large bare patches in Darwin mangroves today remain from the impact of 1974's Cyclone Tracy.

Secretive Chestnut Rails amongst mangroves

Mangrove species commonly observed around Darwin

Club mangrove *Aegialitis annulata*

A low growing shrub to 1.0 m high, occasionally to 3.0 m with a basally swollen, fluted trunk. The bark is dark and smooth with longitudinal fissures and may be flaky on older plants. The twigs are ringed by leaf scars (thus the name *annulata*). Leaves are spirally arranged and clustered terminally on the shoot. Solitary flowers are small and white, appear during September to November and are probably pollinated by ants. The fruits are cryptovivivarous (the embryo begins to enlarge before leaving the parent tree and even before the outer shell is ruptured). The enlarged fruits, or hypocotyls are longitudinal and a crimson colour when ripe. Similar to many mangroves the propagules are well adapted to water dispersal. *Aegialitis* is found in habitats with salinity at or above that of seawater and is common on rocky and exposed shorelines. *Aegialitis* is also found at the landward edge of the mangroves and fringing saltflats.

River mangrove *Aegiceras corniculatum*

A small tree or shrub to 5 m tall with smooth grey to brown bark with numerous lenticels or air-breathing pores. The oval leaves are alternately arranged, thick and leathery with a rounded tip and a whitish undersurface bearing a prominent midrib. Being a salt secretor (a mangrove that exudes excess salt from its system through salt glands) the leaves are often covered with a deposit of salt crystals. Sweet smelling white flowers produced during May-October have five petals that twist to the left. The floating seeds are dispersed by the tide during the wet season. Tolerant of a wide range of salinities, the River Mangrove is found in a variety of mangrove habitats from the landward margin to low clumps fringing seasonally brackish waterways.

Grey mangrove *Avicennia marina*

A widespread species that may be a tree to 15 m or low stunted shrub under poor conditions but mostly a multi-stemmed tree 4 to 10 m high. A conspicuous mangrove species with silvery undersurface to the leaves that may form pure stands at both the landward and seaward fringes. The smooth bark is green to grey, mottled and peels in patches. The numerous pneumatophores (aerial roots) are thin and pencil-like and radiate out from the tree in lines marking the position of underground cable roots. Leaves are elongated, shiny green above with a long pointed tip. The Grey Mangrove flowers from October to February and the small dark orange flowers produce a strong rotten fruit odour. Fruits are rounded and short beaked, around 2 cm long. The fruits are eaten by some Aboriginal groups after extensive soaking and cooking. Capable of growing in many tidal habitats, *Avicennia* is the most widespread and common mangrove species in the Northern Territory. In Darwin it can be seen in most mangrove habitats and is a coloniser of the shores of Vestey's Lake near the Sailing Club.

Bruguiera exarista

A small tree 3 to 8 m high with dense foliage and the trunk has a flanged stem base. The bark is rough, dark grey and fissured in a coarse, regular chequered pattern. Roots produce numerous knee-like pneumatophores. Leaves are glossy, leathery and crowded at the ends of the branches. Yellowish-green flowers with 8 to 10 calyx lobes appear from May to November. Fruits 'germinate' on the plant and the cigar-shaped, pendulous hypocotyls are produced year round. Hypocotyls are 4 to 9 cm long and up to 0.8 cm wide crowned by a persistent cap or calyx. *Bruguiera* is a common species on the landward fringe and in the midzones of coastal mangroves where it typically forms a codominant stand with Ceriops, mid-way between the seaward and the landward fringes. It is thought that the red-headed honeyeater pollinates this species as it visits the flowers for nectar.

Bruguiera parviflora

A slender tree to 5 m tall with grey, fissured bark, a slightly flanged trunk and knee roots to 30 cm high. The elliptic leaves are narrower than those of other Bruguiera species. From June to December, small yellow-green flowers with a ridged cap or calyx bearing 8 small lobes are produced. The cap-like fruit capsule stays attached to the hypocotyl during its dispersal, the new leaves growing and breaking through this on establishment. Hypocotyls that wash ashore onto on the muddy substrate in a horizontal position are actually self-righting. They establish rapidly, putting down an anchor root and then rising into an upright position. Often growing in mixed stands with Rhizophora in the lower tidal zone where it is inundated by most tides.

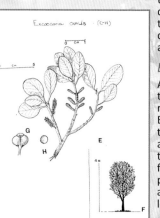

Kapok mangrove *Camptostemon schultzii*

A shrub or tree capable of growing to 20 m but most commonly a tall shrub that often overhangs creek beds in the lower tidal zone. The trunk has grey bark with longitudinal fissures and is often fluted towards the base. In very poorly drained areas it produces knotted roots that protrude above the mud and are covered with lenticels -assisiting in their internal aeration. Leaves are alternately arranged, the undersurface is pale and covered in minute rusty coloured scales. These tiny scales also cover the stem, flowers and fruit capsule. Flowering occurs from June to October and the fragrant white flowers are followed by development of ovoid fruits to 1 cm long. The common name, Kapok Mangrove refers to the dense cotton-like material which covers the the seeds aiding both water and wind dispersal.

Ceriops tagal var. tagal

A shrub or small tree to 6 m with pale bark becoming flaky on the short basal buttresses. In highly saline areas it becomes stunted. Leaves are glossy, rounded and lack a pointed tip. Foliage is thick, leathery and clustered to the ends of the branches. *Ceriops tagal var. tagal* produces flowers in clusters of up to 10 held on slender curved stalks in the late dry season. Like some other mangrove species, *Ceriops* is viviparous meaning that the seed germinates on the parent plant. The emerging embryo looks like a small horn, giving rise to the name *Ceriops* from the Greek 'ceras' (horn) and '-opsis' (appearance). When mature, the slim hypocotyls are between 4-10 cm long and smooth. These are gradually dropped from the tree

to be dispersed by the next tide. Ceriops forms dense single species stands in mangroves in the Darwin region. In Darwin Harbour *Ceriops* covers extensive areas of the tidal flat comprise approximately 40% of the total mangrove area.

Excoecaria ovalis

A semi-deciduous mangrove tree to 4 m tall typically found within the diverse landward fringe of the mangroves. Knotted roots are occasionally found close to the surface but pneumatophores are absent. Excoecaria can be easily distinguished from all other species of mangrove trees by the presence of white latex which is reputed to cause blindness. During November and December partial or complete leaf fall occurs. The rounded leaves may turn a bright red or yellow before falling from the tree which is then followed by flowering and concomitant leaf production. Male and female flowers are tiny and produced on separate spikes up to 4 cm long during October to December. Fruits are small and light brown. Aboriginal people have numerous medical uses for the leaves, sap and charcoal obtained from this species.

Lumnitzera racemosa

A small tree or evergreen shrub with very dark grey to black bark. Bark is longitudinally fissured and the local species has no pneumatophores. Leaves are thick and fleshy and the tip has a notched apex. Leaves are spirally arranged and clumped towards the ends of the branches. The white, tubular, stalkless flowers appear from October to May and are rich in nectar. Small, flattened woody fruits containing a single seed in a fibrous coating are easily dispersed by water and occasionally vast numbers of seeds can be found washed up along the high tide line. *Lumnitzera racemosa* is a common and widespread species preferring the consolidated muds at the landward fringe of mangroves, often growing in association with *Ceriops* and *Excoecaria*.

Stilt-rooted Mangrove *Rhizophora stylosa*

A distinctive mangrove with its extensive network of arching stilt roots and spreading branches with slender aerial roots. Commonly growing as a small to medium tree generally 5 to 10 m high. *Rhizophora stylosa* may reach 17 m locally and forms the tallest mangrove forests in the Darwin region. Bark in young trees is smooth and pale grey becoming fissured or tessellated and black in mature trees. Leaves are elliptic, dark glossy green and leathery. The leaves are much longer than wide, have evenly spaced oil dots beneath and there are prominent leaf scars on the smaller branches. Flowers are composed of white feathery-hairy petals surrounded by stiff waxy lobes. These are borne in clusters on long stalks. Hypocotyls are substantial, pendulous structures with a pointed tip - up to 30 cm in length. *Rhizophora* forms dense single-species stands close to the seaward margin of the mangrove.

Sonneratia alba

A medium to large spreading tree growing to around 10 m in the Darwin region with horizontal or drooping branches and stout conical pneumatophores rising up to 30 cm above the ground. Bark is smooth, cream to brown with fine longitudinal fissures. Many larger trees have extensive hollows which create suitable habitat for marine animals. The opposite leaves are rounded to oval, thick and fleshy. The prominent flowers are composed of numerous, white stamens and are thought to be pollinated by bats. Flowering occurs throughout the dry season Fruits are smooth, flattened globular berries with a long pointed tip enclosing numerous small woody seeds in a thick pulp. *Sonneratia* is a coloniser species that pioneers the unconsolidated mud banks on the seaward margin at around mean sea level. Plants at this point on the shore are inundated by every tide and tolerate conditions similar to marine species.

An underwater glimpse at these mangrove trees

Saltflats

The Top End coast and Darwin's extreme seasonal climate in which annual evaporation often exceeds precipitation, combined with the macrotidal range results in some parts of the intertidal zone becoming extremely salty or hypersaline. In these areas the salinity of the groundwater is too high even for mangroves. Here saltpans or saltflats occur. Largely devoid of vegetation or with scattered samphire including *Batis argillicola* and *Halosarcia halocnemoides*, these areas can be very extensive and are characteristic of the upper tidal zone. Patches of samphire with succulent stems, unusual flowers and an overall bright pink colour can be found in the vicinity of Darwin's East Point Mangrove Boardwalk and are worth a close look.

Coastal Plant Communities

Coastal plant communities in the Top End and Darwin area comprise an interesting group of species that draw from a number of different habitats. Coastal monsoon vine-thicket species may grow in association with strand plants, woodland species and paperbarks on substrates varying from rock outcrops (for example; around the Darwin CBD) to beach sand and poorly drained silty clays at the rear of mangroves.

Common trees

Native Ebony *Diospyros maritima*

A compact evergreen tree usually 5 to 8 m high, noticeable for its dense shiny dark green foliage. The bark is smooth and tight and pale to dark grey. The leaves are oblong to elliptic and up to 20 cm long with wavy margins and paler beneath. The stalkless female flowers are white, bell-shaped and singular. The male flowers are borne on a separate tree, are smaller and clustered. The fruits are round berries growing to the size of a large black grape, changing from reddish-orange to black when ripe. The edible fruits contain 3-4 shiny brown seeds and are eaten by birds especially pigeons.

Dodonaea platyptera

A small evergreen bushy tree 4 to 7 m high with narrow leaves tapering to a point. The bark is pale grey and slightly fissured and the limbs of older trees may be gnarled and slightly twisted. Male and female flowers form on separate plants, are small and greenish in colour, and are a good source of nectar for bees and insects. *Dodonaea* is most likely to be noticed for its winged seed capsules. The seeds are enclosed in a papery capsule 2 to 3 cm in diameter, comprising two wings becoming dry and pale brown when ripe. An abundance of capsules form during March to July and probably assist in the dispersal of the plant by the wind. A common tree on stabilised dunes by the beach extending to low cliffs and fringing mangroves.

Mimusops elengii

A large evergreen tree with an upright growth habit and a dense crown of shiny dark green foliage. The trunks of older trees have rough, tessellated bark from dark grey to black in colour. The alternate leaves are characteristically crowded together, oval and smooth with a prominent mid-rib and short pointed tip. The flowers are cream-coloured, scented and hairy to 1 cm in diameter. Fruiting occurs in April to June when bright red oval berries develop in the leaf axils. *Mimusops* is a common tree on stabilised dunes behind the beach adjacent to mangroves, old beach ridges and on low coastal cliffs. It is a slow growing, stable tree whose qualities have been recognised in its recent introduction to cultivation, now being widely planted as an amenity tree throughout Darwin.

Yellow Flame Tree *Peltophorum pterocarpum*

A spreading tree with lush bipinnate leaves, *Peltophorum pterocarpum* is well known for its profuse fragrant golden flowers. It is a deciduous tree, 10 to 15 m tall with bipinnate leaves 20 to 30 cm long, composed of numerous fine leaflets 1-2 cm long. The bright yellow flowers are displayed above the crown on branching rusty coloured stalks to 45 cm long. Flowering begins around August creating a spectacular display worthy of the tree's common name. The rusty brown woody pods persist on the tree for a long time adding to the tree's generally unruly appearance.

Pongamia *Millettia pinnata*

A dense crowned tree generally 5 to 10 m high with smooth pale grey bark. Pongamia is most noticeable for its very spreading almost umbrella-shaped growth habit. The leaves are pinnate, divided into 2 to 3 pairs of broadly oblong leaflets 5-15 cm long. Each leaflet is a glossy dark green, thin textured and distinctly veined. The cream to pale pink small peaflowers appear during September to November. Numerous flowers are clustered on

stalks within the foliage. Fruits are flattened, woody peapods to 6 cm long containing 2 red-brown seeds. Pongamia is a fast growing, hardy tree, common on dunes behind the beach extending into coastal monsoon vine forest and thicket. All parts of the plant are reported to be toxic and produce vomiting. Nevertheless, oil from the seeds is used in India for various medicinal purposes.

Premna serratifolia

Spreading shrub or small tree typically 2 to 3 m high in the beach dune environment and harsh monsoon thicket sites. The opposite leaves are shiny, leathery, broadly ovate to almost round but quite variable in shape. The leaves have prominent venation with a raised mid-rib underneath, and are deciduous as the dry season progresses. The flowers are small green-cream in much branched terminal clusters 10 to 20 cm across. During May to July smooth globular berries develop, changing from green to black as they ripen. The old branched flower stalks remaining on the tree may be a helpful diagnostic feature. The tree has numerous Aboriginal uses including carving spears from the wood, and the application of heated leaves to marine stings and spear wounds. Widely distributed through SE Asia to India and Japan.

Strand Vegetation

The beaches and coastal dunes of northern Australia have a suite of largely cosmopolitan species. These include the low trees and shrubs Scaevola sericea, the orange-flowered *Cordia subcordata*, the Beach Gardenia *Guettarda speciosa* and the Beach Sheoak *Casuarina equisetifolia*. All of these species are common from Africa through India, Asia and Indonesia. In addition to these are species, which occur in the tropics worldwide. The most obvious of these are the beach hibiscus *Hibiscus tiliaceus* and the purple flowering vine *Ipomoea pes-caprae*.

Strand plants are adapted to a relatively harsh environment - one of salt spray, excessively drained sandy substrate and the occasional drenching by a spring high tide. Some species are quite salt tolerant and many have floating seeds to facilitate their dispersal (eg. *Cordia subcordata*, *Guettarda speciosa* and *Thespesia populneoides*). Unlike coastal monsoon vine-thickets in which the majority of species are deciduous, many strand plants retain their leaves throughout the dry season.

Strand plants perform an important role in coastal stabilisation and several deep rooted vines such as *Ipomoea pes-caprae*, and *Canavalia rosea* virtually bind beach dunes together.

Caesalpinia bonduc

A scrambling shrub 1 to 3 m high, with large bipinnate leaves up to 70 cm long with leaves and stems amply armed with vicious hooks enabling it to climb over other vegetation. During January to April sprays of yellow peaflowers appear on long stalks. Flowering is followed by the formation of spiny oval shaped pods to 6 cm long, each containing two blue-grey, slightly angular, marble-like seeds. The seeds float and remain viable even after several years bobbing around at sea. A pantropic species found on seashores and in vine thickets.

Canavalia rosea

A prostrate dune creeper with 3-lobed leaves, the central leaflet being the largest. Flowers are held on long erect stalks above the foliage. The pretty purple-pink pea-flowers bloom progressively from base to tip. Following flowering, large brown beans develop in woody pods. The beans float, aiding their dispersal. They are edible after boiling - being poisonous when raw. Common on coastal sand dunes above high tide level. Widespread throughout the tropics.

Beach She-oak Casuarina equisetifolia

A tree between 10 to 20 m high, often dominant on coastal sand dunes, beach fronts and low headlands. Graceful spreading habit and rough, dark grey, fissured bark. Easily identified by its fine foliage of drooping needle-like branchlets. The sea breeze makes a whistling noise as it passes through these trees. Male flowers are in small terminal spikes and female flowers are small and globular, later developing into prickly woody cones characteristic of the *Casuarina* group, and often found beneath the tree. Enclosed within the cone are the small papery winged seeds which are known as samaras. *Casuarinas* may form dense stands on coastal foreshores across the Top End.

Sea Trumpet Cordia subcordata

A shrub or small tree with a spreading growth habit 5 to 10 m high. The bark is longitudinally fissured and a cream to grey colour. Glossy ovate to heart shaped leaves are large, 8 to 20 cm long. On close inspection a row of tiny hairs beside the midrib is visible. The attractive orange trumpet-shaped flowers, about 4 cm across, have distinctive crumpled petals and are produced in terminal clusters. The fruit is a round dry woody nut up to 3 cm in diameter, containing 1 to 2 seeds. The seeds are edible. A pantropic species of sand dunes on the foreshore, vine-thickets on stabilised dunes, occasionally at the rear of mangroves.

Beach Gardenia
Guettarda speciosa

A shrub or small spreading tree 3 to 6 m high with smooth, blotchy cream-grey bark. The opposite, broadly ovate leaves are large, 10 to 25 cm long, and crowded towards the ends of the branches. The leaves are smooth above, sparsely hairy beneath, with prominent yellowish veins. The tubular white flowers have 4 - 9 spreading lobes and their delightful perfume is strongest at night and in the early morning. Flowers are held in groups of up to 15, but flowering is sequential with only one or two flowers opening at once. The fruit is a round woody nut that becomes the perfect floating 'buoy' to facilitate its dispersal around the coast or overseas. A strand plant most often found on sand dunes above high tide level or in vine-thickets toward the rear of the beach.

Beach Hibiscus *Hibiscus tiliaceus*

A small spreading tree 5-8 m high with a rather untidy appearance. The large, 15 cm, heart-shaped to circular leaves are whitish and densely hairy on the undersurface. The leaves have prominent raised venation and a short pointed tip. The yellow flowers have dark purple centres and do not open as widely as cultivated Hibiscus. Flowering is periodic and the flower petals turn from yellow to reddish before falling from the tree. Fruit is a semi-woody capsule that splits when ripe releasing several kidney-shaped seeds. Aboriginal people used the wood for carving and making spears, fire-sticks and woomeras. Infusions from the inner bark have antiseptic qualities and the tough bark is suitable for making string, rope, fishing lines and nets. The roots, flowers and young leaves are edible. A coastal species occurring from Africa to the Pacific Islands and tropical America.

Goat's foot Convolvulus *Ipomoea pes-caprae*

A colonising vine of coastal habitats with rapidly growing prostrate stems. *Ipomoea pes-caprae* is a perennial and grows from a thick taproot. The large bilobed leaves are thick and smooth, 4.5 to 12 cm long. The common name derives from the leaves' two equal lobes - which are suggestive of a cloven hoof. Flowering is periodic and the prominent trumpet-shaped flowers have pink to purple thin-textured petals. The fruits are round woody capsules that split open to release 4 hairy seeds. The plant is widely used for medicinal purposes both by Aboriginal people and in SE Asia. The heated leaves are used to treat marine stings, catfish and stingray wounds, aches and lesions.

Scaevola sericea

A common shrub bordering the beach, 2 to 3 m high, with dense foliage and thick fleshy stems. Easily recognised by its shiny, broad leaves being widest at their tips and arranged spirally around the smooth green stems on very short stalks. The flowers are white, 2 to 3 cm long, with a fan-shaped structure. Fruits are smooth, fleshy and slightly pear-shaped enclosing a hard stone. Scaevola sericea is a hardy, salt-tolerant species with a pantropical distribution most often found on the dunes above high tide level or occasionally at the rear fringes of mangroves. It is a useful species for coastal stabilisation work.

Thespesia populneoides

A low growing tree usually multi-stemmed with tight,

smooth, grey bark. The distinctly heart-shaped leaves are smooth and thick, ending in a sharply pointed tip. The undersurface of the leaf has prominent venation and is covered in tiny rusty coloured scales. Fruits are non-splitting woody capsules containing several rounded seeds. Like many pantropic species the fruit is dispersed by floating in sea-water - the seeds may remain viable for many months at sea. Similar in appearance to *Hibiscus tiliaceus* which is in the same family (Malvaceae). *Thespesia* is distinguished by its rusty scales, leaf shape and texture (not hairy). Found primarily on stabilised sand dunes above the beach and in brackish to salty environments including saltflats and the landward fringes of mangrove forests.

Birds of the Mangroves

Mangroves support a rich bird community. In the Top End you can find the Brahminy Kite, Shining Flycatcher, Large-billed Gerygone and particularly Black Butcherbird associated with mangroves.

Mangrove birds tend to have longer bills than their non-mangrove relatives. This seems to be an adaptation which helps avoid the clogging of bills and the muddying of faces when food is picked off the forest floor and from damp, tidally inundated trunks and branches. Also watch for nests disguised as flood debris. At least one bird, the Large-billed Gerygone does this.

A bird to look out for in the late wet season is the Red-headed Honeyeaters, which is normally confined to mangroves. In the late wet season there are virtually no flowering mangroves to support them. At this time you can see the Red-headed Honeyeater in suburban gardens of Darwin, particularly in close proximity to mangroves. In the early wet season, the newly fledged young Red-headeds are dispersing and, again, it is possible to see them in gardens at this time.

During the wet it is possible to see the Cicadabird in mangroves. At this time it is quite common and possibly breeds in this habitat.

The Partitioning of space in the Mangroves

There are several groups of birds where more than one member of a particular genus have taken to the mangrove forests. Four gerygones, for instance, are known to use mangroves. The Mangrove Gerygone is pretty much confined to mangroves and restricts itself to low shrubby mangrove. The Large-billed Gerygone occurs in the same tall, dense forest as the Green-backed Gerygone, but is more widespread and breeds in mangroves. The White-throated Gerygone of the eucalypt forests forages on the landward edge of mangroves, leaving the taller denser forests along tidal creeks to the Green-backed Gerygone.

Other birds, which partition space, are the flycatchers, fantails and whistlers. The Rufous Whistler, a bird of the eucalypt woodland, keeps to the landward fringe of the mangrove. Both Mangrove Golden and White-breasted Whistlers coexist in low, dense shrubs but avoid each other by taking different foods and foraging at different levels in the mangroves.

Great-billed Heron *Ardea sumatrana*
A large, 110 cm, grey brown tropical heron with massive bill. Unlikely to be confused with any other bird. A skulking heron, keeping to the mangrove-lined waterways. Stalks along mudflats for aquatic animals. Voice guttural, loud croak, occasional roaring.

Striated Heron *Ardea striatus*

Small, 50 cm, black-capped heron with back brown-grey, body darker above than below. Metallic sheen. Throat and forehead streaked black. A skulking, solitary bird, sometimes diving onto prey others stalking along feeding on crustaceans, fish , insects and particularly mudskipper. Voice, harsh 'tch-aah', explosive 'hoo'.

Chestnut Rail *Eulabeornis castaneoventris*
Chestnut-bellied 50 cm, with long yellow-tipped green bill and powerful yellow legs. Remarkably shy and secretive, best observed at low tide when they come out of the mangroves to feed on crustaceans. Seen singly or in pairs. Voice, loud raucous trumpeting.

Brahminy Kite *Haliastur indus*

A distinctive white and chestnut hawk, 43-51 cm, of coastal habitats particularly mudflats and mangroves. Brahminy kites are commonly seen soaring along Darwin's coastline including the city and coastal suburbs. A slow-soaring hawk, with a short tail, it is usually seen singly or in pairs. An inoffensive scavenger, it seeks carrion along tide-lines, occasionally seizing fish from the water or small reptiles and insects from the ground eating small prey on the wing. Its call is a stuttering 'pee-ah-ah-ah', feeble trills, mews and squeals.

Little Bronze-cuckoo *Chrysococcyx malayanus*

Small, 15 cm, cuckoo with iridescent bonze-green plumage and broad incomplete bars on underparts. Red eye ring. Parasitises nests of the Large billed Gerygone, others will do also. Solitary and quiet, feeds on insects and caterpillars in the midstrata. Voice prolonged, high pitched, rippling whistle.

TC

Forest Kingfisher *Todirhamphus macleayii*

Blue rumped kingfisher with two-toned blue upperparts, white windows in wing, large white spot before the eye. Black stripe from bill to ear coverts. Underparts buff. Seen sitting still, staring down intently for prey which it pounces on. Voice harsh trilling chatter of repeated notes 't'reek t'reeek.

Little Kingfisher *Alcedo pusilla*

Tiny, 12 cm, short-tailed kingfisher, upperparts blue, with white breast. White spot before the eye. Australia's smallest kingfisher, it is solitary and unobtrusive. Spends most of its time perched on a low branch over water, looking fixedly down. It dives to seize tiny fish, crustaceans etc. Voice is a shrill whistle.

Collared Kingfisher *Todirhampus cloris*

A green-rumped kingfisher, 28 cm, with white underparts, green and blue back, small white spot before eyes, white underparts. Lives mainly on the seaward fringe of mangroves, spaced out singly or in pairs. Usual perch and pounce strategy, but does not dive into the water, rather snaps prey up from the surface. Voice, double note 'kik kik' repeated three of four time in rapid succession, far carrying.

Lemon-bellied Flycatcher *Microeca flavigaster*

Brown-tailed flycatcher, 12 cm, with yellowish underparts, upperparts olive-brown. Working from the midstrata, it hawks out to catch insects alone or in pairs. Voice, glorious sweet clear varied song 'quick quick come with me'

Mangrove Robin *Eopsaltria pulverulenta*

Greyish robin with white underparts with a greyish wash to upper sides of breast, 15 cm, has black lores, white bases to outer tail feathers. The Mangrove Robin keeps within the lower mangroves in small, sedentary family groups. Work from the midstrata and also wait and watch to pounce on insects and crustaceans on the mud. Voice, long mournful double note.

TC

Mangrove Golden Whistler *Pachycephala melanura*

Male, striking looking, yellow breasted with a black head, white throat and yellow edges to wing feathers, back olive-green. Female plain grey-brown with undertail coverts yellow. About 15 cm. Inhabits the taller mangrove forest, where it forages solitarily or in pairs through the middle strata. Hops methodically amongst branches and occasionally drops down to mud to pick up crustaceans. Voice, melodious loud, persistent and clear whistling notes 'chee-chee-chee-tu-whit'. Like a whip cracking at end.

Broad-billed Flycatcher *Myiagra ruficollis*

About 15 cm. Male head and cheeks glossy blue-grey, chin throat and upper breast rufous orange. Underparts white. Female is paler. Both have small erectile crest. Established pairs are sedentary in the interior of mangroves at mid strata. Birds forage alone by hawking and sallying through this level. On perches, they sit upright, quivering their tail, raising their crests, and calling sporadically. Voice a repeated whistling 'too-whee'.

Large-billed Gerygone *Gerygone magnirostris*

Small bird, 10 cm, with warm-brown head and upperparts. Underparts cream-white, washed cinnamon on breast. Brown eye. Large-billed keeps to the taller stands of mangrove. Has a heavier bill than the Mangrove and may take harder shelled insects. Sedentary, singly or in dispersed pairs. Voice descending reel of three or four notes.

Mangrove Gerygone *Gerygone tenebrosa*

Brown backed, 10 cm, with white eyebrow, red eye, white in tail tip. Forages for insects, gleaning amongst the foliage, lower in the canopy than Large-billed. Sedentary, singly or in dispersed pairs. Voice series of rising and falling whistled chromatic cadences.

Red-headed Honeyeater *Myzomela erythrocephala*

Dark brown honeyeater with unmistakable red head and rump, about 12 cm. Female not as red. Mostly confined to mangroves where they wander locally in ones and twos. Take insects and nectar within the mid and upper strata. Voice, harsh whistles, metallic jingling twittering.

Yellow White-eye *Zosterops lutea*

Yellow-breasted small bird, 11 cm, with short pointed bill and ring of white feathers around the eye. Upperparts olive-yellow. Move nomadically throughout the outer foliage branches of mangroves in groups or 30 or more. Glean for insects on leaves and twigs. Voice rapid, loud warbling song.

Black Butcherbird *Cracticus quoyi*

Whole body of this large butcherbird, 44 cm, is bluish black. Sedentary, established pairs are territorial. A bird of rainforest and mangroves, Black Butcherbirds forage through all strata of the forest. In mangroves will walk about at low tide foraging for crustaceans. Hunting alone the birds will dive or probe for insects, eggs, frogs, reptiles, even fruit. Voice is a loud, quick clonking. Song a repetitive fluting yodel.

Black Bittern *Ixobrychus flavicollis*

Male bill black above and yellow below. Upperparts sooty-black; side of neck yellow. Underparts white with prominent brown and black streaks down neck. Dark brown blotches on breast and belly. Female upperparts brown, not black. Found in mangroves and small creeks in forests.

Mammals of the Mangroves

Water Rat *Hydromys chrysogaster*

This large aquatic rat lives near permanent water and sometimes on beaches. It usually has dark fur on the back, paler underneath, and a white tip to its tail. It grows to about 300 millimetres, and has partially-webbed hindfeet. It eats large aquatic insects, crustaceans, fish and small mammals.

JB

Flying Fox

Mangroves are the favoured day-time haunts of flying foxes, two species of which are found in the Top End and Darwin area. The Little Red is dark reddish-brown and grows to about 235 millimetres, and has transparent wing membranes. The larger Black Flying-fox is black all over with a reddish collar, and grows to 260 millimetres. In natural areas, they eat native blossom and fruit, but in orchards eat fleshy fruits, particularly mangoes.

Flying Foxes are naturally fairly mobile species, and move according to their food supplies. In the evening, they can be seen in thousands heading inland towards their favourite crops of blossoms or fruits. While feeding and roosting, they can set up quite a din with their squabbles.

Little Red Flying Fox *Pteropus scapulatus*

Black Flying-fox *Pteropus alecto*

JB

Reptiles of the Mangroves

There are a number of fascinating reptiles to be found in the mangroves. Some of the most distinctive are described below.

Black-ringed Mud Snake *Hydrelaps darwiniensis*

The most colourful sea-snake in the Darwin area is the Black-ringed Sea snake, with its bright yellow and black bands right along the body and its paddle-like tail. It grows to about 50 cm and is found mostly on mudflats and in mangroves. Forages for fish along rising and falling tidelines.

Intertidal Skink *Cryptoblepharus littorea*

This is the only skink in this region, known to have adapted to living beside freshwater and sea water.

White-Bellied Mangrove Snake, *Fordonia leucobalia*, eating a crab.

Mudskippers

Small, goggle-eyed fish that don't seem to like water, mudskippers are to be found on muddy beaches, mangrove mudbanks and tidal flats. Their large, protuberant eyes, like little periscopes searching the skies for predators, have lower eyelids. The mudskipper uses its pectoral fins like oars, pulling the body along behind. The tail fin is lifted up to reduce drag. From this folded position, it can also be used like an uncoiled spring making the fish flip, skip or hop. Uniquely for a fish, the mudskipper can climb trees such as the prop roots of mangroves.

Strangely enough, mudskippers can drown if kept submerged for too long. To breathe, the mudskipper takes a breath of water with air, shutting its mouth and spreading its small pouch-like gill chamber. This makes the fish look like it is puffing out its cheeks. The water moistens the gills and the air allows the fish to respire. In addition the mudskipper can breathe directly through its skin which is fed by a fine net-work of blood vessels, especially in the tail. Mudskippers dig their burrows with their mouths.

There are 10 species of mudskipper in the Northern Territory. Three species in the genus *Periophthalmus* are the most commonly seen mudskippers. They grow to about 100 mm in length and eat small crabs, insects, spiders and marine worms. *Boleophthalmus* is another commonly seen genus, represented here by two species. These are big mudskippers, growing up to 250 mm. They have broad, coloured dorsal fins and feed by straining through soupy mud, moving their heads from side to side, filtering out fine algae, diatoms and tiny animals. *Boleophthalmus caeruleomaculatus* is a big, common species with brilliant blue spots. It displays to other mudskippers by leaping up and down, using its body as a spring.

The long, thin mudskipper, *Scartelaos histophorus*, is another mudskipper you might see. It does not leap up and down, preferring to row along in soft, semi-liquid mud where it feeds with its narrow dorsal fin carried straight up.

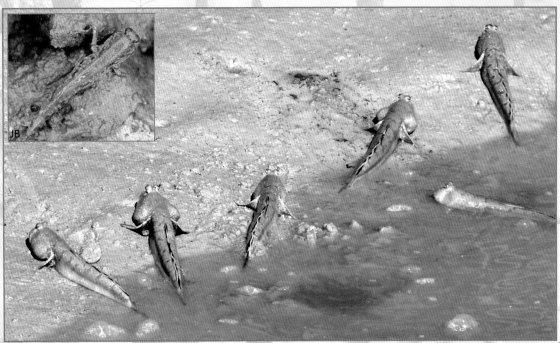

Crocodiles

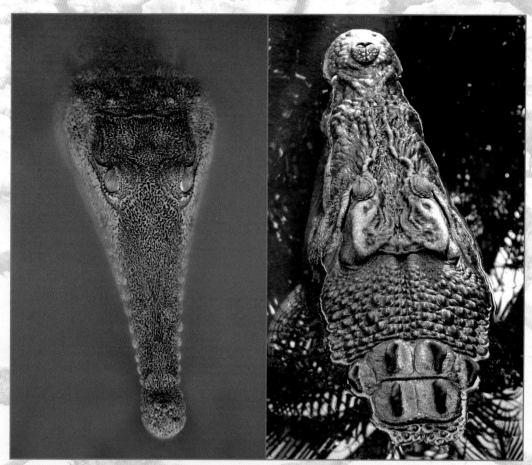

Crocodiles are awesome creatures. The largest living reptiles in the world, they are also ancient. In fact, the ancestors of crocodiles appeared around 200 million years ago and belong to a group of archeosaurs, or "ruling reptiles", which included the dinosaurs and the ancestors of birds (which are just feathered archeosaurs). At this time some crocodilians were immense with skulls (leave alone the rest of the body) of 1.5 metres. They probably preyed on dinosaurs. As fantastic as it seems, the closest relatives to crocodiles today are in fact birds. In many ways parental care is similar to that of birds with nest building and care of the young hatchlings.

There are 27 species and subspecies of crocodilians in the world. Australia has two, *Crocodylus johnstoni*, the freshwater crocodile and *Crocodylus porosus*, the so-called salt-water crocodile. In fact this crocodile, which preys on humans amongst other things, penetrates well up into freshwater areas, and large numbers are found in some totally freshwater lagoons and swamps. Keep this in mind when visiting inland waterways.

Saltwater crocodiles are distributed from India, through South-east Asia, the Solomons and Vanuatu. Throughout most of this range, they are still hunted for hides. The Australian population is the stronghold of the species.

Male "salties" mature at about 16 years of age when they are about 3-4 metres long; females when they are 10 years of age, when they are about 2-3 metres long. They nest in the wet season, from November to April, laying about 50 eggs in vegetation and soil mound about 15 cm high. The female guards the eggs for the three month incubation period and assists in the release of the hatchlings, often by taking them gently in her mouth.

Crocodiles bigger than about 2.5 metres, are big enough to attack a human. Crocodiles are conservative feeders, however, and prefer barramundi, wallabies and a variety of other prey. The very large crocodile

As floodwaters recede in the late dry months crocodiles can get caught without water and are known to bury themselves in the mud until the flood waters return. Often crocodiles will bury themselves by choice.

A Freshwater Crocodile hatchling

"Sweetheart", which is exhibited in the Darwin Museum, had pig bones, long-necked turtles and barramundi in its stomach when it was caught.

In contrast to the saltie, the "freshie" is only found in Australia, and usually in the upper freshwater reaches of rivers. Males mature at 2 m and females 1.5 m when both are about 12 year of age. Again, in contrast to the saltie, freshies nest during the dry season. It is a highly synchronised affair, and takes place towards the end of August and early September when a hole in the sand is excavated. Incubation is about 3 months and females dig out the nest at hatching time. Freshies don't pose such a threat to people but they do resent being walked or jumped on. So, you need to exercise some care when sharing some of the upland plunge pools with them.

To distinguish these crocodiles note that the Saltwater crocodiles have 2 rows of enlarged nuchal shields. They are grey to almost black with darker mottling. Freshwater crocodiles have 1 row of enlarged nuchal shields. They are grey to brown with darker bands. (Refer to page 166) for differences in jaw and head structure.

CHAPTER NINE

The Sea

The Darwin and Top End coast lies at the confluence of the Timor and Arafura Seas, shallow, warm seas, which are rich in nutrients and ideal for growth of many marine species. Because the seas are shallow, there are no major upwelling currents bringing cool deep waters to the surface, such as on the Great Barrier Reef and the Western Australian barrier reefs. As a result we have a different and particularly interesting group of corals and sponges, which are a mixture of Indian and Pacific Ocean and southern Asian species.

Hard Corals

Soft Coral

Darwin Harbour has sponges, corals and a seahorse, which are found nowhere else. Over 300 species of coral are found in the waters off Darwin, and even more sponges are known to occur here. Whip corals - long strands of sometimes colourful corals that look like plastic tubing - live in the active zones of the fringing reefs, particularly at East Point. In fact, a stroll along the rocky foreshores at Lee point, East Point and Channel Island will reveal a wealth of fish, sponges, shellfish, crabs, corals and other marine species. Whip coral's dead remains are made of keratin, the same material as hair, and are occasionally found washed up on beaches, looking like dead sticks. Try breaking one, and the difference will be obvious. Whip Corals are incredibly tough, so tough in fact that they are valued as material for jewellery.

Australian Anemone Fish *Amphiprion rubrocinctus*

False Clown Anemone Fish *Amphiprion ocellaris*

On the rock shelfs at Lee Point, East Point and Channel Island, anemones and anemone fish provide colour and life to the reefs. The anemones, attached to the rocks, live a symbiotic existence with algae, called zooxanthids, and produce the vibrant colours, the pinks, blues, reds and yellows splashed among the corals and sponges. Clown fish, those harlequin players flitting amongst the stinging anemones, have a special relationship with the anemones. They ingest the stings of the anemones and become immune over time to the anemones, using them for protection from predators, and in return eat the unwanted algae and microscopic plankton that would otherwise smother the anemones.

Anemone

Anemone

False Clown Anemone Fish, black & white banded form

Mushroom Coral

Stone fish, deadly, almost invisible and motionless, lie in wait amongst the rocks for an unwary fish to come cruising past. Their dorsal spines contain poison enough to painfully kill an adult person, and are quite capable of penetrating a thong or sandshoe. Care is needed when wandering among the rocks and corals looking for the beautiful nudibranchs and shells. Nudibranchs are carnivorous soft-bodied animals which swim and crawl over the rocks. Their soft fringe-fans and gelato-like colours are astonishing, and worth a search.

Stonefish, Darwin Harbour

Sea Cucumber *Holothurus atra*

Makassan fishermen have been visiting these shores for 600 years or more, hunting and collecting trepang, or beche-de-mere. Amongst the rocks, one particular species of trepang, also known as sea slug, is common - the Black Sea Cucumber *Holotheria atra*. While the Grey Sea Cucumber was preferred for its size and taste, the Black was also collected, salted, dried, smoked and sold to Chinese buyers in Indonesia.

Tritons, Bailers, and Cowries live among these rock shelfs. Unfortunately, many are collected so it is sometimes difficult to find them. Not so the enormous variety of Ascidian worms such as *Lissoclinum patella* and *Botrylloides* species, which are found on all the rocky shores in great and colourful variety. Careful observation may also reveal fan corals (also known as Gorgonians because of their many-headed appearance), such as those at Lee Point, and Feather Stars on Gorgonians. The Feather Stars are nocturnal, so only display at night while they filter the water currents for planktonic food.

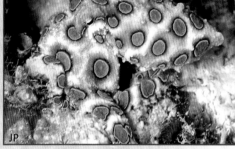

Blue-ringed Octopus, genus *Hapalochlaena*

Blue-ringed Octopuses clamber over many of the rocks, and exquisite Weedy Sea Dragons are occasionally seen at places like East Point. Soft corals, some of the most colourful of the rock-dwelling creatures, including the *Dendronepthya*, as well as Milky Oysters also live along the sea coast at Lee and East Points. A chaos of fish provides frenzied life to the rock shelfs. Blue Damsels, Freckled Pufferfish, Blue-streaked Rockskippers, Scribbled Angels, Beaked Coral Fish, Cardinalfishes and Lattice Soldierfish are among the variety to be found on these shores. Lucky observers may see Blue-spotted Rays off shore or while snorkelling, and the (mostly harmless) Black-tipped Reef Sharks cruise silently by these reefs.

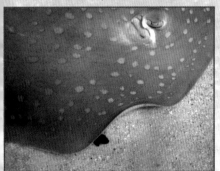

Blue-spotted Ray *Neotrygon kuhlii*

Freckled Pufferfish

Blue Devil *Chrysiptera cyanea*

JB

Mangrove Jack *Lutjanus argentimaculatus*

JB

Sooty Grunter *Hephaestus fuliginosus*

Good eating fish are caught along the shores of Darwin and the Top End. Spotted Mackerel, Sooty Grunter, Tarpon, Sleepy Cod, Riflefish, Trevally, Mangrove Jacks, Catfish, Sock-eye Salmon, Saratoga, and of course the famed Barramundi live in secret places along the coast. Barramundi in particular have an interesting life history (see box). Clown Fish (or Anemone Fish) undergo a similar change, one male transforming into a female when the dominant group female dies.

JB

Rendahl's Catfish *Porochilus rendahli*

Goose Barnacles are small shrimp-like animals, contained in a tough shell. When the tide rises, their plates open, and the barnacle protrudes its feathery legs, which grasp about like delicate hands in search of food. When the tide falls, the plates close, sealing the animal in its shell with enough water to prevent death, until the sea rises again.

Goose barnacles are filter feeders. They can attach themselves to flotsam that can be found washed up on beaches. If you find them, have a look at these interesting communities and leave them for the tide to take back into the sea. They are still alive.

Goose Barnacles

Goose Barnacles

Oysters on the rocks

The Elusive Barramundi

Barramundi *Lates calcarifer*

One of the animals that epitomise the Top End is the Barramundi. It forms the basis of commercial, recreational and subsistence fisheries and can grow up to 150 cm and weigh as much as 40 kg. A famous fish of north Australia, it is, in fact, widely distributed. It has a coastal distribution from eastern Africa, through Asia to eastern Australia and southern Japan.

In the Top End the fish inhabits rivers, lakes, billabongs, estuaries and coastal waters. Though you may not think so, after a day of fruitless fishing, Barramundi actually dominates many tropical rivers. This is because of its dynamic and flexible biology. Highly fertile fish spawn at river mouths, lakes or lagoons or in open coastal areas where salinity levels are reduced by inflowing fresh water. Eggs hatch rapidly after spawning, usually after no more than 18 hours and the larvae are actively feeding a day later. By the 15th day, larvae can tolerate completely fresh water, and they begin to exploit flooded wetlands adjacent to river mouths. Such rapid larval and juvenile development, which includes a move from almost marine to freshwater conditions within two weeks, is unusual for fish.

Perhaps more unusual is the fish's extraordinary habit of changing sex in mid-life. The larvae continue their journey upstream in their first year where they stay until mature. When they are about 3 years old, still all mature males, they move downstream to the estuary to spawn. Barramundi are amazingly fertile - one scientific record was a female of 124 cm with 46 million eggs! At 6 or 7 years of age, all the males change sex to female (and reap the best of both worlds). The separation of juveniles, which all migrate upstream, from adults may be an adaptation to reduce cannibalism, not uncommon in the piscivorian world.

Angler's luck may be influenced by the barramundi's habits. Most anglers fish in the upstream sections of the rivers in the Top End, the haunts of the smaller male fish.

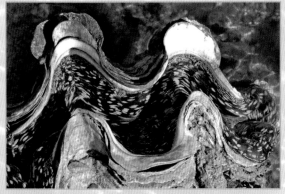

Colourful Giant Clam found on the reefs

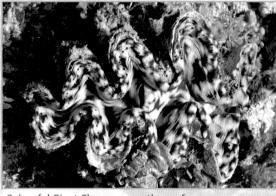

Colourful Giant Clam seen on the reefs

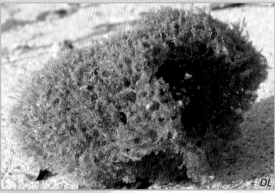

Sea Sponge washed up on the beach

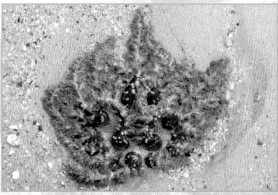

Beach Anemone

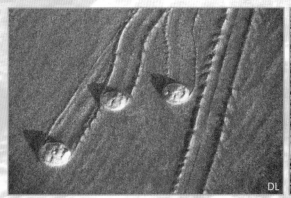

Live Sand Dollars *Clypeasteroida sp.*

A Sand Dollar endoskeleton

Sand Dollars are a type of Sea Urchin which live in shallow tropical waters. If you are lucky you may see live Sand Dollars moving across the sand with the tides or washed up endoskeletons which look like shells.

Spider Shell with a resident

Green Rock Crab

Hermit Crab

Ghost crabs are shy and retreat quickly down the burrows formed at low tide

This Mangrove Crab specialises in eating fallen mangrove leaves

The mud crab favours the estuaries around Darwin.

Look out for the Soldier Crabs marching across the sand at Lee Point, Casuarina beach

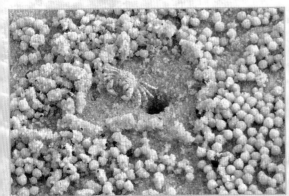

Sand Bubbler Crabs work hard to pattern the beaches around Darwin at low tide.

If you quietly sneak around the rocks you may catch sight of these comical Fiddler Crabs.

But not all is benign. Apart from Stonefish and Blue-ringed Octopi, Tiger Sharks, fierce predators of the coast and ocean, breed in the shallows at Lee Point, while Hammerhead Sharks slice the waters off these shores. Both are deadly. The more insidious Box Jellyfish is perhaps the most worrisome of the marine creatures. It is almost invisible to swimmers, and common during the wet.

Across the Top End, the Box Jellyfish keeps people out of the water from October to May when they emerge from rivers and creeks, with their arsenal of rapidly active venom considered to be amongst the most deadly of all animals. The bell of the Box Jellyfish is a rounded, colourless box shape, difficult to see. In adults the bell can be over 20 cm or so across, and in juveniles less than five centimetres. Fleshy appendages at each corner trail 40 or more tentacles that can be three metres in length. The tentacles have millions of nematocysts that inject venom. Unlike other jellyfish, Box Jellyfish have true eyes and hunt their prey of fish and crustaceans by propelling themselves actively through the water at one or two metres a second - much faster than the average swimming person.

From time to time, headlines are made with strandings of whales on the Darwin region coast. False Killer Whales, a smaller version of and different genus from the Orca, are seen at Cobourg Peninsula, and strandings of a Blue Whale, the ocean's largest ever mammal, have been recorded at Cape Hotham. As recently as 1993, a Sperm Whale was found beached at Casuarina Beach, and in 1995 a Dwarf Sperm Whale was found at Mindil Beach. The Northern Territory Museum collected and preserved the specimen - a whale of a task! Spinner Dolphins are frequently seen off the coast, and in the bow wave of larger boats and ships, while Bottlenose and Common Dolphins are regularly encountered.

The Box Jellyfish
Chironex fleckeri

Sousa chinensis Dolphin with calf

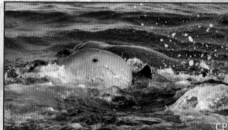

Northern Snub-fin Dolphins *Orcaella heinsohni*

Indo Pacific Bottlenose Dolphins *Tursiops aduncus*

The mythical mermaid is embodied in the Dugong or Sea Cow, a heavy-set marine mammal which feeds on the extensive sea grass beds of the local shallows. Old tales of mermaids are interpreted as sailors' longing for their womenfolk - seeing in the shallow waters these voluptuous creatures and fantasising about them.

Dugongs are regularly seen across the Top End and in Darwin harbour, as near as Mindil Beach, sometimes with their young travelling close beside them. So too are turtles. Five of the six species of marine turtles found in Australian waters frequent the Darwin coastline. Flatback, Olive Ridley and Hawksbill Turtles are the most commonly seen. A major breeding ground for Olive Ridley Turtles is found off the north-east Arnhem Land coast, only a few hundred kilometres to the east. Green Turtles are regularly seen, although the larger Loggerhead Turtle, with its massive head and large body is less common. Several of these endangered species, including the Hawksbill, Olive Ridley, Flatback and Green Turtles nest on nearby shores.

Dugong *Dugong dugong*

Loggerhead Turtle *Caretta caretta*

Green Turtle *Chelonia mydas*

Olive Ridley hatchling *Lepidochelys olivacea*

Turtles and dugongs are two of the relatively few creatures to feed on seagrasses. There are several large seagrass beds in the Darwin region. One located just offshore from the Casuarina Coastal Reserve, another bed not far from the sleepy seaside resort at Mandorah and also within the harbour near Channel Island. Seagrasses grow in small clumps amongst coral reefs or in vast aquatic meadows in adjacent areas. Seagrass meadows are often composed of several species as well as algae. Seagrass beds, like the neighbouring mangrove environment, are extremely productive ecosystems, exceeding the productivity of a comparable area of agricultural land. However, unlike algae or seaweeds, few animals aside from sea urchins, some molluscs, turtles and dugongs actually consume seagrasses.

Sea Urchins amongst seagrass, the Dugongs and Turtles feed on this grass.

Mick Guinea, is the Turtle expert on the Bare Sand Island Project near Darwin, picured with a Hawksbill Turtle

177

A Field Guide to Reptiles of the sea

A note on Sea Snakes

It is uncommon to encounter sea-snakes, even though they can be extraordinarily abundant in some areas. Nearly all sea-snakes are poisonous, but only some are deadly. They are occasionally washed up on shore after storms and may appear to be dead, while still capable of a dangerous bite. They are fish eaters.

Stokes' Sea Snake *Astrotia stokesii*

DANGEROUS. Stokes' Sea-snake is uniformly cream to almost black, although it may have a reticulated pattern on the back. This snake is thick, one of the largest and bulkiest of all sea snakes. It is occasionaly seen in Darwin Harbour, and grows to around 1.2 metres, and up to 2 metres. It is usually seen on the surface in murky waters.

Olive Sea Snake *Aipysurus laevis*

The most common sea snake in the NT and abundant in the corals of

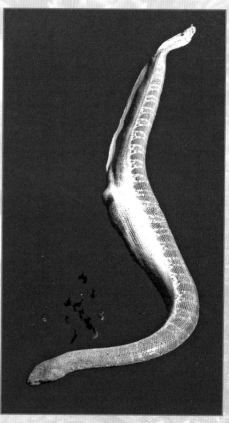

the north. A curious snake, care should be taken by divers waving it away since its bite is poisonous.

Black-ringed Mud Snake
Hydrelaps darwinensis

This colourful sea-snake is endemic to northern Australia and southern New Guinea.

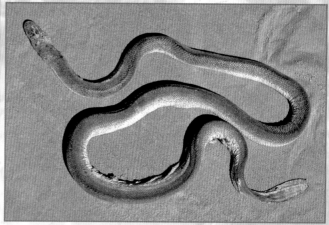

The Beaked Sea Snake
Enhydrina zweifeli

This uncommon sea snake is extremely venomous and can be aggressive. It is responsible for most recorded deaths and injuries from sea snakes.

Hawksbill Turtle *Eretmochelys imbricata*

This endangered turtle has a sharp curving beak hence the name hawksbill. It has a richly patterned carapace and grows to about 1 metre. It can be seen around the Darwin region. Elsewhere in the world, they are harvested for their beautiful shell from which the name tortoiseshell is derived.

Olive Ridley Turtle *Lepidochelys olivacea*

JB

This turtle is usually olive-grey to grey, without pattern. It grows to 1.5 metres. It is common in northern waters and can be seen near Darwin. It occasionally nests on nearby beaches, and a rookery occurs near Cobourg Peninsula.

Loggerhead Turtle *Caretta caretta*

This carnivorous turtle has a massive head, hence the name loggerhead. Its powerful jaws crush hard shelled marine creatures. They prefer deeper water near coral reefs, along the Northern Territory coast.

Flatback Turtle *Natator depressus*

Endemic to tropical continental shelf waters of Australia and the most common marine turtle in the Darwin region is the Flatback Turtle. It grows to about 1.2 metres, and is identified by its flattish back, upturned carapace edges, and thin, fleshy skin over the carapace. It is grey or pale green to olive above. Flatbacks prefer murky inshore waters and nest on associated beaches.

Green Turtle *Chelonia mydas*

This wide spread turtle is olive-green on the back, usually with a pattern of reddish-brown to black. The carapace is high-domed and edges of the carapace are not upturned. It grows to about 1 metre and nests on offshore and island beaches. It is mostly herbivorous as an adult. It prefers clearer offshore reef waters.

PART THREE:
A Field Guide to Localities
of the Darwin Region

Darwin Esplanade

The Esplanade was surveyed and designated as open space by G.W. Goyder, in 1869. It is essentially a strip of coastal cliffs between Doctor's Gully and Government House.

The exotic gardens of the Esplanade

Heading north along the Esplanade you will find Admiralty House on the corner of Knuckey Street. The exotic garden around Admiralty House was established in the 1920s by F. Bleeser, an amateur botanist. This historic

Beauty Leaf
Calophyllum inophyllum

garden includes a Frangipani, Beauty Leaf, Indian Mast and a Raintree that were all planted in the 1960s. The Beauty Leaf, *Calophyllum inophlum*, is a handsome native tree distribued through northern Australia, south-east Asia and India, with large glossy leaves and fragrant white and yellow flowers. The nuts produce a scented, high quality oil which is used in lamps and burners in southern Asia. Aboriginal people used a mixture of ground nut kernels and red pigment to treat body pain.

Large *Calophyllum inophyllum* in the Park near Parliament House in Darwin.

Raintrees, *Albizia saman*, are native to South America, these beautiful shade trees have short massive trunks which can support a canopy more than 30 metres across which erupts in fluffy pink and white flowers early in the Wet Season. The dark brown seed pods contain an edible, licorice flavoured pulp, the newly ripened pods of which are used as fodder for stock in many countries. Elsewhere in the world, the tree drips like rain in the mornings when the leaves open, releasing their reservoirs of condensed moisture. This does not happen in Darwin's climate.

Darwin's Raintree Park, in Knuckey Street, is also shaded by a couple of magnificent raintrees.

Raintree, *Albizia saman* in Darwin's Raintree Park, Knuckey Street

Over the past ten years many Allosyncarpia ternata, an evergreen shady tree from western Arnhem Land, have been added to the list of street species around the city. Two former Lord Mayors were keen to see these iconic trees in the Darwin street scapes. Later in the year these spectacular flowering trees attract many birds and insects and the scent of the flowers is delightful as it drifts on the night air.

Allosyncarpia ternata in the Darwin City Mall

Allosyncarpia ternata in bud

Field Guide to the monsoon forest of The Esplanade

Further along the Esplanade, in pockets along the cliffs, are examples of remnant coastal vegetation. A total of 165 plant species have been recorded here including about 40 exotic species, including the invasive Coffee Bush, *Leucaena leucocephala* and the Coral Vine, *Antigonon leptopus*. Despite the substantial woody weed invasion and some indiscriminate clearing, these remnant pockets remain valuable high diversity habitats in close proximity to the city.

Monsoon vine thicket edging the Esplanade and the path to Lameroo Beach

Common Esplanade plant species described below can also be seen at East Point Reserve and Casuarina Coastal Reserve.

Ficus virens Banyan or Strangler Fig (see pg 104)
Peltophorum pterocarpum Yellow flame tree (see pg157)
Terminalia microcarpa (see pg 108)
Myristica insipida, Native Nutmeg (see photos below)
Alstonia actinophylla, Milkwood (see pg 66)
Mimusops elengi (see pg 156)
Celtis philippensis (see pg 110)
Diospyros calycantha (see pg 104)
Drypetes deplanchei (see pg 110)
Flagellaria indica (see pg 105)
Smilax australis (see pg 107)
Pachygone ovata (see photo right)

Refer to the habitat chapter, particular monsoon forest, for identification of the birds that might be sighted along the esplanade. The monsoon forest pockets have active Orange-footed Scrubfowl nests within them.

Many of the cliff side trees pre-date the settlement of Darwin. Being seasonally dry, these monsoon forests are largely dominated by deciduous species. There are also a variety of semi-deciduous and evergreen trees that help make up the general canopy to 10 metres in height, with the tallest trees reaching 15-17 metres tall. Lameroo Beach in particular has the densest vegetation with prominent clumps of Bamboo, Rock figs and Banyans. A walking track to Lameroo Beach winds down through the shady hillside jungle, past mossy seepage zones and webs of aerial fig tree roots to a small protected beach. Splendid views of the harbour and glimpses of jungle and coastal birds add to the delights of this walk.

Pachygone ovata vine

Jungle chook, (Orange-footed Scrubfowl) mound

Native Nutmeg, *Myristica insipida*. The red mace, referred to as the aril, wraps around the seed of *Myristica insipida* like thin spaghetti (left & right)

East Point Reserve

East Point Reserve is a fine example of coastal monsoon rainforest associated with dry sites. There are well over 100 species of plants including those described for the Darwin Esplanade. The area is extensively used for bushwalking and bird watching. A coastal walk including a boardwalk meanders through the majority of the habitats that have been discussed in this book including seasonally dry monsoon forest, woodland, strand vegetation on chenier ridges and mangroves.

Several mangrove zones are traversed by a boardwalk. From land to sea, a zone of mixed species intergrades with a narrow tidal-flat zone dominated by *Ceriops tagal var. tagal* (see pg 154). Then a taller Rhizophora forest (see pg 155) with its looping, arched prop roots ends abruptly at the margin of the sea dominated by the aged and gnarled trunks of *Sonneratia alba* (see pg 155) trees. The stamenous, flowers of *Sonneratia* only open at night and are pollinated by bats.

Mangrove boardwalk East Point

Orange-footed Scrubfowl

A number of Sandalwood trees, *Santalum album*, a locally uncommon species famous for its fragrant timber are found along the East Point track and represent the largest population in the Darwin environs. Populations of Agile Wallaby and Orange-footed Scrubfowl also inhabit the East Point area.

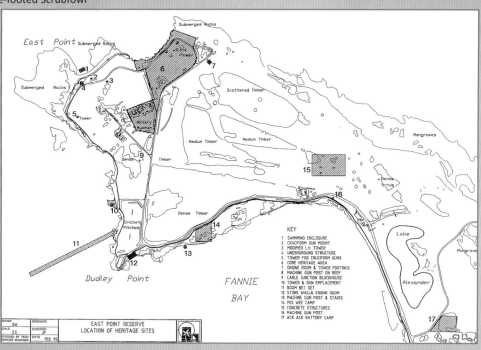

Charles Darwin Reserve

A view across the mangroves to Darwin city from Charles Darwin Reserve

This area is bounded on the north by Tiger Brennan Drive and by Darwin Harbour mangroves on all other boundaries. It includes plateau surfaces, steep sideslopes, lower slopes, drainage floors, and intermarginal areas bordering mangroves.

The area contains largely intact habitats - particularly with regard to the woodland environment and forms an extensive, continuous tract to the east with the Hidden Valley and Rifle Range plateaus, slopes and drainage floors. The open forest tracts are representative of the dominant plant community of the entire Top End. Open elevated plateaus with *Corymbia bleeseri* woodland range to fine, well structured Eucalypt open forest and allow views of the mangroves, the harbour and sometimes Darwin city. Small patches of regenerating monsoon forest occur within the woodland, but frequent fire prevents their full development.

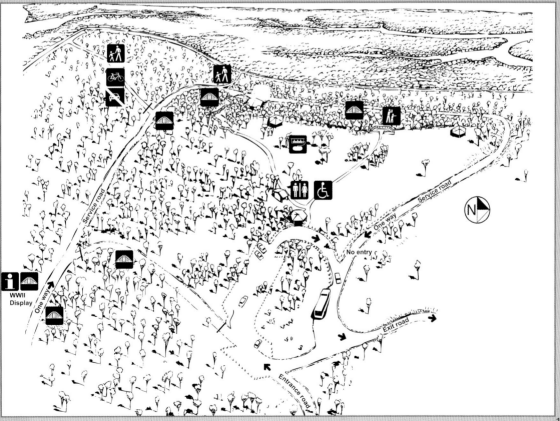

Casuarina Coastal Reserve

An easy walking track winds from Lee Point beach carpark through a shady monsoon vine thicket. It passes through paperbark forest and Casuarina trees that whistle with the wind and from where you can glimpse the sea and access the beach at many points.

Continuing, a board-walk takes in the mangrove communities and mudflats active with crabs. As the track weaves along you can see monsoon vine thickets on sand dunes edging the mangroves. All along there is a diversity of birds associated with the different habitats The track ends at Free Beach carpark.

Monsoon Vine thicket and Mangroves fringe Casuarina Coastal Reserve

Lee Point Beach - Buffalo Creek

A belt of coastal monsoon vine-forest stretches along the western margins of the Buffalo Creek mangrove community. A local rehabilitation program aims to halt the deterioration of this forest. The uncommon tree, *Berrya javanica* occurs here. This is also a well known bird watching area.

Berrya javanica

Mangroves lining the mouth of Buffalo Creek

Rapid Creek

From source to mouth, Rapid Creek represents a unique freshwater ecosystem within the Darwin suburban area, containing a variety of communities and habitats including mangroves, monsoon vine forests, Pandanus, woodlands and Melaleuca or paperbark swamps. From the headwaters of Rapid Creek at the airport, beyond Amy Johnson Drive, to the mouth where it joins the sea is a distance of only 8 km.

Stands of *Melaleuca viridiflora* (see pg 129) and *Pandanus spiralis* (see pg 127) at the headwaters of Rapid Creek indicate seepage zones and areas of seasonal inundation. This plant community merges with surrounding Eucalyptus woodland typical of upland areas of the Darwin region generally.

A monsoon forest community occurs on the creek banks and in places extends up to 50 metres from the creek. Dominant species include the Darwin Black Wattle, *Acacia auriculiformis*, Milkwood, *Alstonia actinophylla* and *Lophostemon lactifluus*.

Other important species include *Melicope elleryana*, Freshwater Mangrove, *Barringtonia acutangula* and *Maranthes corymbosa*.

Freshwater Mangrove flower
Barringtonia acutangula

Holmes Jungle

JRS

Sustained by spring fed Palm Creek, Holmes Jungle is the largest wet rainforest patch of its kind in the Darwin area. Signposted walking tracks and interpretive signs take you through the 256 hectare park. An outstanding jungle, with dense canopy cover, thick leaf litter, abundant palms and buttressed, lichen covered tree trunks. This combined with flowing water creates a lush fertile environment, dominated by evergreen species with ferns carpeting the ground layer.

DL

Field guide to the common monsoon plants

Syzygium nervosum (see pg 107)
Calophyllum sil (see pg 103)
Horsfieldia australiana (see photos below)
Carpentaria acuminata (see pg 104)
Livistona benthamii (see pg 106)
Stenochlaena palustris (see pg 106)

DL

Horsfieldia australiana flowers

DL

Horsfieldia australiana

LEGEND

- **P** Parking
- Toilets
- Picnic Area
- Drinking Water
- Walking Track
- Lookout
- Horse Riding and Cycling Track
- Sealed Road
- Unsealed Road
- Horse Riding and Cycling Track
- Walking Track

Fire break trail

Palm Creek

Fire break trail

Jungle Picnic Area

Hilltop Picnic Area

Gates Open 7 am - 7 pm (closed during wet season)

One way

Two way

To Shoal Bay Recycling Centre

Gates Open 7 am - 7 pm

Main Entrance

Vanderlin Drive

Berrimah →

Karama

Casuarina

N

0   100   200
metres

Fogg Dam

A 3.6 km walk with interpretive signs is a definite highlight of any trip to Fogg Dam. Taking approximately 2 hours, the dominant plant communities traversed are closed canopy Melaleuca forest, Monsoon forest with dense stands of the palm *Livistona benthamii* (see page 106) fringing the edge of the freshwater floodplain habitat. A raised boardwalk allows year-round access through the seasonal swampland and facilitates an appreciation of the radical changes in water regime from wet to dry. This award-winning boardwalk has been designed with sensitivity - being constructed around the trunks of numerous trees.

Magnificent examples of Leichhardt Trees, *Nauclea orientalis* used by Aboriginal people for making canoes and paddles, the edible cluster fig, *Ficus racemosa* (see page 105) with its huge buttressed roots and the tall canopy species *Terminalia microcarpa* (see page 108) can all be appreciated from the track. Some massive woody vines swing from the canopy and have created some fascinating shapes in the trunks by squeezing the small trees they have used to climb there. Thick mosses grow on the flaky bark of *Lophostemon lactifluus* and unusual stalked, cup-shaped fungi arise from rotting branches on the forest floor.

Dragonfly

Leichhardt flowers *Nauclea orientalis*

Some massive scrub fowl mounds up to several metres high occur on either side of the track, and the owner builders can be seen scratching around nearby. The 'walk to work' calls of the stunning Rainbow Pitta resonate through the forest and sitting quietly for a few moments might allow a glimpse of the vivid black, red and blue plumage of this jungle bird. The calls of orioles, drongos and the rufous shrike-thrush echo through the forest canopy. During the wet season the boardwalk takes you into the delightful aquatic environment of the wetlands - suspended over waterlilies and reeds beneath the shady canopy of massive paperbarks. Here, you can quietly observe the activities of frogs and fish, dragonflies and waterbirds.

Territory Wildlife Park

It is worth visiting the Territory Wildlife Park to encounter some of the wildlife and habitats of the Top End. The Park is set on 400 hectares and displays three main habitats; Woodlands featuring patches of Old Growth Eucalyptus tetrodonta forest and includes one of the few areas of this important wildlife habitat protected within a reserve. A visit to the Nocturnal House will reveal the night-time secrets of many woodland creatures. You can also find the endangered northern quoll, Dasyurus hallucatus.

Northern Quoll *Dasyurus hallucatus*

In the Monsoon Forest habitat you can stroll through a series of small aviaries and head into the spring-fed forests where the crystal-clear Berry Springs can be viewed from the boardwalk. You will see massive buttresses on *Ficus racemosa* and *Syzygium nervosum* trees and several large orange-footed scrub fowl mounds along the forest walk. The forest contains two rarely seen species of threatened orchids and is seasonally host to large colonies of the much maligned forest pollinators - the flying foxes.

The wide buttress of a *Syzygium nervosum* tree stands beside the Spring

Wetlands are the third major habitat featured and there are several locations where different kinds of wetlands can be seen. The Billabong is a permanent water body with Pandanus-lined banks surrounding this overflow channel of Berry Creek. The Billabong has islands where water monitors and freshwater crocodiles may be seen sun baking. From the rotunda, over the water, you can watch the turtles swimming and Pelicans cruising around the water waiting for Tucker-Time.

Australian Pelican *Pelecanus conspicillatus*

The Aquarium gives a special underwater perspective on waterways of the Top End from the sandstone escarpment springs, down the creeks and rivers and out to the coral reefs offshore. Insights into freshwater sawfish conservation research and sustainable fisheries are included here.

The Peregrine Falcon *Falco peregrinus* features in the Birds of Prey daily shows

For the bird twitchers, and others who prefer a low-key experience, there is Goose Lagoon. A natural lagoon surrounded by dense paperbark forest that is flooded during the Wet Season and evaporates in the Dry. Highlights include the spectacular sight of a monsoonal downpour across the already flooded lagoon, huge flocks of magpie geese that rely on these areas as the landscape dries, and the deafening chatter of honeyeaters when the *Melaleuca viridiflora* trees are flowering.

Berry Springs Nature Reserve

Berry Springs Nature Reserve adjoins the Territory Wildlife Park and shares the spring that feeds into the refreshing pools where people swim. The creek has a clear blue green colour from the spring water. It is fringed by a monsoon vine forest gallery of trees.

There are many freshwater fish, so take your mask and snorkel. There is a series of natural pools and the reserve has shady picnic sites, barbeques and tables. You can take a lovely short circuit walk through the monsoon forest. You may even be lucky to see a Rainbow Pitta.

Channel Island

Channel Island is connected to the hinterland via the Elizabeth River Bridge. The island has had an interesting history, including being the site of the Darwin leprosarium and now the location of the gas fired power station that supplies Darwin with electricity.

The island is fringed by one of the best coral reefs in Darwin, that can be readily appreciated by a well-timed walk over the intertidal zone during a low spring tide. The reef is particularly renowned for its variety of soft corals, sponges and sea fans.

The rocky shores of the island exposed to the prevailing North-westerly winds during the monsoon, have some outstanding examples of wave sculpted rocks. In the more protected embayments and rocky shores mangroves occur.

Looking from the Channel Island bridge into the Mangroves

References

Brennan, K. (1986) Wildflowers of Kakadu. Published by Kym Brennan, PO Box 568 Jabiru, Northern Territory.

R.Booth, R.K.Harwood, C.P. Mangion (2011) Field Key for the Monsoon Rainforest Flora of the Darwin Region. Published: NT Herbarium.

Braby Michael(2004) The Complete Field Guide to Butterflies of Australia. CSIRO Publishing

Braby Michael (2011) 'New larval food plant associations for some butterflies and diurnal moths (Lepidoptera) from the Northern Territory and eastern Kimberley, Australia '.
The Beagle, Records of the Museums and Art Galleries of the Northern Territory, 2011 27: 85–105

Brock, J. (1994) Plants of Northern Australia. Reed Books, Australia.

Clark Mike & Traynor Stuart & Dunlop Adi (1987) Plants of the Tropical Woodland.
Conservation Commission of the Northern Territory.

Cogger Harold G. (1992) Reptiles and Amphibians of Australia. Reed Books.

Cogger Harold G. (2014) Reptiles and Amphibians of Australia. (seventh edition)
CSIRO Publishing.

Cole, J. & Woinarski, J. (1994) A Field Guide to the Small Mammals of the Northern Territory. Key and Species Descriptions for Rodents and Dasyurids. Conservation Commission of the Northern Territory, draft Mss.

Crowder, B. (1995) The Wonders of The Weather, Bureau of Meteorology.

Dunlop, C.R., Leach, G.J. & Cowie, I.D. (1995) Flora of the Darwin Region. Northern Territory Botanical Bulletin No 20. Conservation Commission of the Northern Territory, Darwin.

Horner P. (1991) Skinks of the Northern Territory. Handbook Series No. 2. Northern Territory Museum, Darwin.

Liddle Dave, et.al. (1994) Atlas of the Vascular Rainforest Plants of the Northern Territory Commonwealth of Australia.

Morris Ian, (1996) Kakadu. Steve Parish Publishing.

Petheram, R.J & Kok, B (1986) Plants of the Kimberley Region of Western Australia. University of Western Australia Press.

Pizzey, G. (1980) A Field Guide to the Birds of Australia. Angus and Robertson. Sydney.

Russell-Smith, Whitehead, Cooke. (2009) Culture, Ecology and Economy of Fire Management in North Australian Savannas. CSIRO Publishing.

Schodde R. & Tidemann S. (1986) Readers Digest complete book of Australian birds. Readers Digest Services, NSW.

Shine, R. (1991) Australian Snakes. A Natural History. Reed, Sydney.

Slater, P, Slater, P & Slater, R (1986) The Slater Field Guide to Australian Birds. Rigby. Sydney.

Storr G.M., Smith L.A., & Johnstone R.E. (1981) Lizards of Western Australia. I. Skinks. University of Western Australia Press with Western Australian Museum.

Storr G.M., Smith L.A., & Johnstone R.E. (1983) Lizards of Western Australia. II. Dragons & Monitors. Western Australian Museum, Perth.

Storr G.M., Smith L.A., & Johnstone R.E. (1990) Lizards of Western Australia. III. Geckoes & Pygopods. Western Australian Museum, Perth.

Storr G.M., Smith L.A., & Johnstone R.E. (1986) Snakes of Western Australia. Western Australian Museum, Perth.

Strahan, R. (Ed). (1983) The Australian Museum, Complete Book of Australian Mammals. Angus and Robertson, Sydney.

Thomson, Bruce (1991) A Field Guide to Bats of the Northern Territory. Conservation Commission of the Northern Territory. Government Printer. Darwin.

Tucker, M. (1989) Whales and Whale Watching in Australia. Australian National Parks and Wildlife Service, Canberra.

Tyler, M.J. & Davies, M. (1986) Frogs of the Northern Territory. Conservation Commission of the Northern Territory, Darwin.

Tyler, M.J., Smith, L.A., & Johnstone, R.E. (1994) Frogs of Western Australia. Western Australian Museum, Perth.

Wightmann, G. M. & Andrews, M (1989) Plants of Northern Territory Monsoon Vine Forests Vol.1. Conservation Commission of the Northern Territory, Darwin Australia.

Wightmann, G. M. (1989) Mangroves of the Northern Territory. Northern Territory Botanical Bulletin No 7. Conservation Commission of the Northern Territory, Darwin.

Wilson S.K. & Knowles D.G. (1988) Australia's Reptiles. Collins, Sydney.

Map supplied by Parks and Wildlife Commission NT © Northern Territory of Australia and is distributed under Creative Commons Licence http://creativecommons.org/licenses/by/3.0/au "

Map on page 8 / Chapter 1: The Pine Creek Geosyncline came from Bureau of Mineral Resources Geology and Geophysics, Bulletin 82.
Paper by Dunn, Randal, Skwarko and Hays. 'Geology of Katherine-Darwin Region, Northern Territory'

Murray, Peter (1987). Plesiosaurs from Albian aged Bathurst Island Formation siltstones near Darwin, Northern Territory, Australia. The Beagle, Records of the Northern Territory Museum of Arts and Sciences 4(1): 95-102.
Murray, Peter (1985). Ichthyosaurs from Cretaceous Mullaman Beds near Darwin, Northern Territory. Australia. The Beagle, Records of the Northern Territory Museum of Arts and Sciences 1985; 2(1): 39-55.

Carrington, Richard (1960) A Biography of the Sea. Publisher: Chatto & Windus, London.

Diagram 5 on page 36 / Chapter 3 is from a paper by Tapper, Nigel (2002) 'Climate, Climatic Variability and Atmospheric Circulation Patterns in the Maritime Continent Region' pg. 9 from book, Bridging Wallace's Line. Published by, Catena Verlag, Germany

Wilson S. & Swan G. (2003). A Complete Guide to Reptiles of Australia. Published by Reed New Holland.

To learn more about Gulumoerrjin (Larrakia) seasons, visit www.larrakia.csiro.au for a downloadable seasonal calendar.

Index